overcoming form: reflections on immersive listening

Richard Glover & Bryn Harrison

Published by University of Huddersfield Press

University of Huddersfield Press
The University of Huddersfield
Queensgate
Huddersfield HD1 3DH
Email enquiries university.press@hud.ac.uk

First published 2013
Text © The Authors 2013
Images © Mike Walker

Every effort has been made to locate copyright holders of materials included and to obtain permission for their publication.

The publisher is not responsible for the continued existence and accuracy of websites referenced in the text.

All rights reserved. No part of this book may be reproduced in any form or by any means without prior permission from the publisher.

A CIP catalogue record for this book is available from the British Library.
ISBN 978-1-86218-120-5

Printed by The Amadeus Press,
            Cleckheaton, West Yorkshire.

COVER IMAGE:
© Mike Walker

Contents

Acknowledgements		1
Introduction		3
Chapter 1	Sustained tones, sustained durations Richard Glover	7
Chapter 2	Performed installations Richard Glover	29
Chapter 3	Repetitions in extended time: recursive structures and musical temporality Bryn Harrison	41
Chapter 4	Listening through Morton Feldman's *Triadic Memories* Bryn Harrison	61
Bibliography		75
Recommended listening		81
Biographies		85

Acknowledgements

The authors Richard Glover and Bryn Harrison would like to thank: Graham Stone, Information Resources Manager, Computing and Library Services, University of Huddersfield, who provided essential project support and also all the staff at Jeremy Mills Publishing Ltd. In particular, we would like to thank Mike Walker for his contribution of artwork and Tim Rutherford-Johnson for his outstanding and thorough work as copyeditor. Finally, we would like to thank musicologist Bob Gilmore for giving permission to use his term 'overcoming form' for the title of the book.

Introduction

The last fifty years have seen an abundance of composers exploring the construction of works that encourage what might be considered an immersive form of listening. The majority of writings on this subject so far have focused upon analytical models based upon original scores and influences behind the pieces. This book is, however, centred solely on the experience of the listener. It aims to expand this area of knowledge through a series of writings that can be viewed as investigations into how listeners not only *hear* sonic environments, but also perceive and *experience* them, and how they respond to the specific compositional devices used by composers in their creation.

It is this awareness and comprehension of our surrounding environment through bodily perception to which we allude when we describe 'experience'. The book explores the independence of the listener in immersive environments that inspire greater autonomy and responsibility. By immersive environments, we mean a global continuity within the sounding environment: an auditory situation in which it is not specifically the artwork, but also our manners of comprehending its nature, that gives meaning to the experience. Immersive listening corresponds to this act of comprehension in these environments.

The group of chapters that follows can be seen as sitting somewhere between two monographs, and an edited collection of essays. The chapters are written very much from the point of view of practitioners working within the field, and in each the authors reflect in very different ways on musical works that could be said to deal directly with the experiential, immersive nature of listening. Both composers share a long-held fascination with the perceptual aspects of musical temporality (including issues such as duration-as-experienced and event time-ordering) and these interests are inevitably reflected both in their own compositions and in the content of these essays. Many of Richard Glover's works utilise sustained tones as their primary/sole material and his two chapters similarly concern issues of temporality, spatial awareness and a sense of an 'evolving' auditory apparatus. Bryn Harrison's music, on the other hand, deals very directly with repetition and cyclic forms. This is reflected in the coverage in his chapters of recursive musical structures and our auditory memory. Both authors believe that their practical knowledge as composers is important in enabling an understanding of the reasons *behind* the construction of the music under discussion, and how this relates to the listeners' experience. Issues of temporality, memory and recall are woven into the discussions to enable further understanding of how we process music over a given timescale.

Intentionally, each chapter does not begin from a starting point of theoretical knowledge, but rather deals with the author's own personal encounters with the music under discussion. In some cases it has then been necessary to include external viewpoints in order to illuminate ideas; however, it should be emphasised that the book does not attempt to provide a comprehensive coverage of the field. Neither does it attempt to provide, from a musicological/analytical standpoint, a detailed construction of the pieces discussed. Issues of construction are undoubtedly important, but in this case rather than leading the discussion they colour it. As the book's title suggests, the focus rather is on the reflective or perceptual process of listening itself, which may, or may not, involve some degree of contextual underpinning. The phenomenological work on perception and temporal experience carried out by Merleau-Ponty is drawn upon where appropriate to illuminate how these experiences fit into a wider context of experiential philosophy, thus enabling further avenues of thought and exploration.

The book is separated into two sections. Each author has provided a longer chapter that deals with aspects of immersive listening but places it within a larger framework for discussion, as well as a second, shorter chapter that applies this thinking to a more directly experiential account of a piece. Each of the four chapters, however, is intended to be exploratory in its outlook and it is important to stress the first-hand subjective nature of these comments. As the different viewpoints adopted by each of the author's testifies, the book acknowledges that every person's experience of music and account of time passing is different and based upon their perceptive responses while listening. Indeed, even for the authors, their response to listening to the works under discussion may have been different if they had been experienced at a different time or in a different environment. It should also be considered that an account of these works can never replace the first-hand experience of listening itself. What is hoped is that the reader might see this book as an invitation to follow up and reflect on some of the examples given, and to explore some of the resulting commonalities and differences in perception. For this reason, a list of recommended listening is given at the back of the book.

Such a book can never account for all approaches to making music that deal with extended presents and immersive auditory environments. Most of the examples used in Richard Glover's chapters on sustained-tone music, for instance, focus on composed rather than improvised forms of music. Similarly, Bryn Harrison's chapter on repetition avoids a larger discussion of areas of musical repetition such as are found in musical minimalism or certain forms of world music. Such a survey could be considered beyond the realms of such a short book. Instead the authors choose to focus on just a few pieces in each chapter as a way of illuminating certain works that seemed pertinent for discussion, based on the author's own preferences, or that have had a direct influence on their thinking as composers.

Finally, the book also contains reproductions of visual work by Mike Walker. These six prints (including the cover image) were commissioned especially for the book. Walker is a visual artist with a particular interest in contemporary music whose work similarly engages with issues of scale and immersive properties. He has collaborated on several occasions with Bryn Harrison. The images serve to emphasise the reflective nature of this book as well as provide a different perspective on the written work.

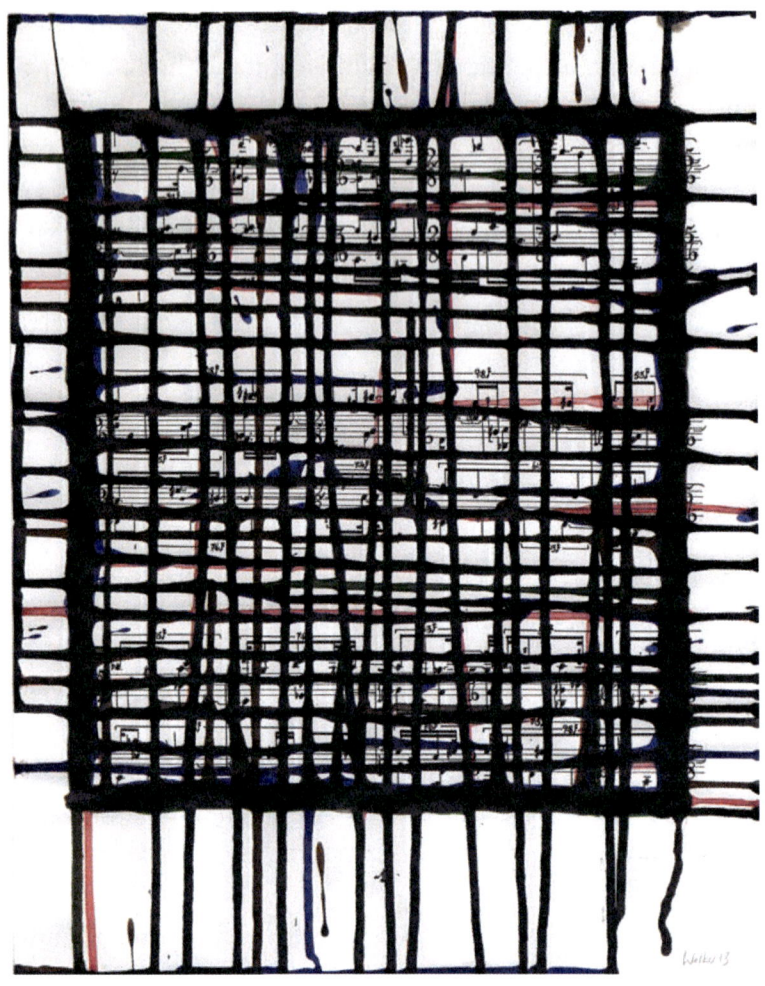

© Mike Walker 2013

Sustained tones, sustained durations

Richard Glover

For me, the sustained tone is a powerful tool for deployment in extended, immersive environments. Sustained tones provide us with a unique landscape upon which expectancies, imaginations and temporalities can be flexible and entirely individual. These pitches are continuous, promoting an experience of extended presents. They can provide a much-enhanced appreciation of the effects of sound on our auditory systems, memory processes and our being as a whole; they can prompt to us examine our way of understanding the world at a greater level.

This chapter will explore the human experience of sustained tone music, and the role our perceptual and cognitive processes play in this experience. Throughout the chapter, I use the phrase 'sustained tone' where others may use the word 'drone'; drones are often understood as a somewhat redundant form of musical information, or, as Joanna Demers describes them, a form of sensory deprivation (2010, 93), that allows a heightened performance from perception by prompting the listener to attend to nuanced variations in the surface of the sound, which in turn gain a greater significance. Whilst I align with the latter half of that statement, the former projects the notion of inertia and a fixed pitch (in terms of construction, rather than the experience of audition), and to some degree, therefore, a fixed experience. However, what this chapter argues is that the transformational nature of the material, the extended duration and the subjective experience all lead to evolved auditory and cognitive processing, rather than a 'redundant' view of the material.

A common feature of discussion around sustained tone music is that individual pieces are often grouped together under very general headings or issues; however, once individual composers and pieces are explored, it becomes clear that there are widely varying experiences to be gained from the different approaches taken. This provides the impetus to describe individual pieces throughout this chapter, as emphasised in the introduction, so as to avoid these generalisations and investigate specific instances, thereby allowing a more rigorous approach. Individual composers and individual pieces can communicate individual intents, which should be ascertained to illuminate the discussion and provide further insight. I aim to give enough context for each piece to lead the reader through the discussion, but I do not analyse the construction of the music in great detail (except where it illuminates an argument); rather, it is the experience of listening to the results of that construction, throughout the duration of the piece, which is of primary concern.

Listening

> [W]hen the sounds are very long ... it can be easier to get inside of them. (Young 1965, 81)

La Monte Young has made a lifetime's work of investigating music of this type. Sustained tones invite their own particular listening mode, or modes, which prompt the listener to comprehend the music, and their relationship to it, for themselves. This approach is less what the theorist Ian Quinn calls 'quarendo' (to obtain, to get), which is familiar to more traditional compositional syntaxes, and more what he calls 'audiendo invenietis' (to discover on hearing) (2006, 287). It is an environment in which to discover the manner in which music is built and performed, and more significantly how it is experienced. The cellist Charles Curtis, when considering the sustained tones and acoustic phenomena of Alvin Lucier, considers the role of the listener as a pro-active, performative agent:

> [T]he listeners, or audience, due to the perceptual challenges posed by the music, are placed in a sort of performing posture, actively seeking

out these borderline effects that are by no means obvious or spotlighted. (2012, 3)

Curtis's comments stem from his vast experience of playing music by Young, Eliane Radigue, Terry Jennings, and Alvin Lucier, amongst others, and reflect his feeling that listeners and performers share the crucial act of listening, which he sees as being central to the act of music-making itself. He also makes the claim that performing is itself a listening event, but a listening infused with the engaged and active focus of performance. The roles traditionally reserved for the performer and listener are reversed, and Curtis intriguingly points towards Young's *Composition 1960 #6*, in which performers act as audience, wherein their perceptual processes (not just the auditory) are heightened to a degree beyond that of the audience observing them. In sustained tone music, the listener is tasked with perfecting their auditory art throughout the duration, and to perform at a high level for edifying results.

Much of this ties in with recent theoretical work undertaken by the psychologist Alva Noë, who argues that we should consider the role of our perception in terms of the sense of touch: a haptic approach to perceiving the world. Most often, the visual and aural senses become the mandatory representations of the perceptive processes, and we quickly acclimatise to what the consequences of our perceptions working in this manner are: the act of passively *receiving*. However, when perception becomes an *action*, a reaching out, or a searching, then the actual process of gaining information by perception shifts responsibility to the perceiver, rather than external sources *providing* sensory information to the individual, who then receives. We enact our perceptual content through a skillful activity of the body. This powerful concept helps frame our perception in a much more pro-active manner, and only helps to reinforce Curtis's comments concerning the performative nature of listening – the 'seeking out' and 'handling' of auditory material to be processed. When framed in this way sound assumes a more tactile form that the listener is able to grasp at will, and sustained tones provide a form of decentralised landscape in which the sounds are there to be grasped freely.

Rytis Mažulis

I begin this exploration of enacting our auditory processes with *Ajapajapam* (2002), a piece for mixed choir, string quartet and sine tones by the Lithuanian composer Rytis Mažulis. Over its 35 minute duration the piece provides a sustained immersive environment in which close pitch clusters within the choir and string quartet generate harmonics that interact with the continuous sine tones at a higher pitch. The cellist Anton Lukoszevieze states that the piece gets to the very core of what it can mean to 'listen' as opposed to just hearing music (quoted in Janatjeva 2006), and I aim to expand upon his observation to elucidate exactly what it is about a sound environment such as this that can engender a more concentrated approach to listening.

The voices' and strings' sustained tones meld together and soon lose a strong sense of either identity, as focus shifts to tracking the changes in density created by the continual entries for individual singers, which are then lost as they enter the global sound mass. Occasionally, individual voices rise out of the texture, but then quickly recede; we again perceive the homogenised nature of the pitch clusters. From this, our own sense of curiosity impels the performative act of our listening to detect more within the sound, so as to satisfy our perceptual processes in the intensive listening environment of the concert hall. Once we adopt this active, performative listening, we are able to perceive repetition, pattern development and gradual transformation within the sound, both from the various fundamental pitch and harmonics, and the resultant beating patterns generated by the clusters. The relationship between the voices and strings, and the sine tones feels as though in continual adaptation; whilst the sine tones maintain a clearly separate timbral field that can be parsed from the voices and strings, the rhythms of their beating patterns occasionally meld with the beating patterns from the voices and strings. Active listening, a reaching out to touch the auditory environment and pull apart the separate strands, can at once hear pure octave unisons between the sine tones and choir, or intervals just wider than octaves, or the multitude of beating pattern layers within the sine tones themselves. The close tone clusters become difficult to parse into single tones until pitch intervals expand past the critical band (the intervallic range in which two pitches cannot be parsed); however, individual perceptual systems interpret this differently, resulting in widely-contrasting individual experiences as clusters form and dissipate uniquely in individual auditory systems. This fuzziness in perception is intriguing: there is not one single ideal of what this piece is, as each participant experiences it in their own individual manner.

The higher sine tones of *Ajapajapam*, and the manner in which the harmonics of the singers and strings interact with them, provide considerable transformation throughout the piece, as do the dramatic changes in densities (albeit gradually). This clearly points to what psychologist Bob Snyder has termed 'articulations', suggesting that small parametric changes do not constitute major sectional boundaries, but rather articulations within those boundaries. Snyder uses the term 'syntax' to define sets of relations between identifiable patterns, and we can therefore perceive that syntax generated by different beating patterns in Mažulis's piece. The syntax is in continual transition, as articulations appear at sporadic moments dependent entirely on performers, instruments, room acoustics and so on.

When beating patterns, density, pitch strands and other parameters remain stable for a short duration, a sense of the present extending is brought about. When an articulation then occurs, that feeling subsides and we 're-perform' our listening approach appropriately for new beating pattern speeds, or whatever it may be that the new articulation brings. When articulations appear infrequently, we experience an 'extending' of the present, which seems to derive from the specious present, a time period of roughly three seconds during which we are able to perceive all incoming data before it is transformed into memories in our short-term memory. I am not suggesting that the specious present itself extends, but if there are sections of, say, six seconds wherein no perceivable articulations occur, then the overlapping specious presents may well be experienced as an extended continuum. These moments certainly occur within *Ajapajapam*, and since our performative listening approaches drive a heightened sense of awareness, we are then likely to become more aware of this localised lack of articulation for this short duration. Focusing on the temporality of that time period results in its being experienced as longer.[1]

Jonathan Kramer notes that what he calls 'vertical music', which would include *Ajapajapam*, does not provide clear chunking cues, resulting in the music's seeking to 'defeat memory' (1988, 336). Whilst the chunking cues require higher demands from the listener's perceptual processes, they are still evident in *Ajapajapam*, as articulations – it is simply a case of adapting to each piece's individual auditory environment.

What is clear when experiencing this music is the difficulty of recalling specific articulations, separate from others; Merleau-Ponty states that 'the present experience has, in the first place, to assume form and meaning in order to recall precisely this memory and not others' (1962, 20), and in low-information scenarios such as *Ajapajapam*, the form and meaning of each of these various present experiences are much more difficult to distinguish, and lead to problems in the recall process. This consequently reinforces the difficulties with distinguishing and recalling similar experiences from the past. However, when we recall a recent articulation, this constitutes what is known as 'rehearsal', which reinforces our memory's ability to store and recall that articulation correctly.

What I find is that these memories accumulate, and I am able to compare memories with each other and with the presently perceived articulations. However, what I find powerful is that this accumulation of memory prompts

---

[1] Richard A. Block concluded that activities that included an attention to time have a strong influence on perceived length – making it appear longer. See Snyder (2000, 214).

me continually to discover *new* patterns within the sound; to be able to discover the new, I must have an idea of what has already occurred, so that, to some degree, I am able to recognise it as a pattern that I have perceived before. It becomes increasingly difficult to maintain any standardised time-ordering capabilities with these memories; they act not as indicators of a timeline, but rather as reference material, which become increasingly difficult to parse between in recall due to their similarities. Whilst I may not be able to recall the precise sound of that articulation, I can certainly recall what Curtis calls the 'experience of sound' – the feeling of the articulation, the knowledge that these articulations occurred.

As I strive to discover the new patterns, I have to ascertain how I can reveal them: I start to touch and untangle the various threads, uncovering new articulations, all the time comparing them with varying degrees of accuracy with what has already occurred. The continual accumulation of all these articulation memories prompts me to conceive of new ways to listen to the sound, and consequently acquire a greater understanding of my own perceptual processes. I perform my listening, I reach out into the sound, and in so doing, its ability to parse, store and recall articulations improves. In this way, 'listening' begins to include more than the interpretation of auditory information, both perceptually and cognitively. It involves memory and anticipation, evolving knowledge and heightened perceptual processes informed by comparative recall. Curtis describes the process not as ear training, from the traditional musical-familiarity exercises, but rather 'mental training', a kind of developed aural analysis (2012, 6).

As these articulations are very much part of the surface layer of the auditory environment, the process of listening to *Ajapajapam* occurs against a ground of the sustained textures of the voices, strings and sine tones. This aural continuity of the background is less timbral, as the spectral palette is often intertwined with the surface layer articulations. Rather, it is a constant *guide* for the global pitch shape of the piece. The shape is a significant aspect; whilst it is difficult to perceive motion in the shape at any one moment due to both the extremely gradual pitch change and the focus towards the surface layer, I do experience the shape over a certain longer duration, as a result of this continuous background texture. Whilst the ordered structuring of the surface articulations is difficult to comprehend due to the small variances between them complicating memory recall, the global pitch shape can be comprehended through memory much more easily ('the pitch cluster I am experiencing now is lower in pitch then before' / 'the pitch cluster descended steadily throughout the piece'). At points where endurance may result in my active, performative listening receding, I find myself experiencing this background pitch continuum; *Ajapajapam* has a global pitch shape that descends over a perfect fifth throughout, and the use of pitch clusters means that it is only the beginning and end that employ octave unisons between the different parts, therefore ensuring that the pitch clusters do not bring focus upon themselves throughout the duration until the end, as the size of the pitch clusters remains largely continuous throughout. The ability to comprehend this type of shape, and yet simultaneously focus on the surface layer, is what phenomenologist Don Ihde names the temporal focus: he states that the 'narrower the focus, the more the background recedes into a fringe appearance' (2007, 90). The shape is so continuous and simple in *Ajapajapam* that although it remains in the fringe it is still comprehensible. Sculptor Robert Morris has stated that the simpler the shape of an object, the stronger the gestalt, as basic forms appear more whole and unified than complex ones. Despite the duration, the basic shape of the pitch cluster of *Ajapajapam* can be perceived as a whole, unified object, both during and after the experience.

This concern of a singular, global shape to *Ajapajapam* recalls sculptor Donald Judd's remarks that works of art 'should have a definite whole and maybe no parts, or very few' (quoted in Lippard 1968, 154). His own approach to structure was against the idea of setting up relationships between contrasting parts, as he wanted to sustain the idea of the entirety: '[t]he whole's it' (1968, 154). A music that creates little sense of variation or development in construction, where homogeneity overrides contrast, is a music that tends towards being perceived as a whole. This can lead the listener to focus on various aspects of the music that often go unnoticed when there are a number of parts.

In a similar vein, composer and theorist James Tenney has said: 'I think of form as the same thing, on a larger temporal scale, as what's called content on a smaller scale' (quoted in Young 1978, 16). This reflects the tendency in some of Tenney's music to focus on the exploration of a single gesture, and how its formal shape is created directly from the material. *Having Never Written a Note for Percussion* (1971) consists of a single dynamic swell performed tremolando, usually played on tam-tam, over a 'long time' (often fifteen minutes or more). The swell is the formal shape, in that there are no other structures present in either the local material level, or at a global level: the form is the content. Mažulis builds a simple formal shape in *Ajapajapam*, which then allows for the smaller articulations to be perceived.

This relates to some degree to what James Tenney would call Temporal Gestalts (Tenney, 1988), which are sections of varying sonic parameters. These are different to articulations, however, as they are understand as implying a distinct change in the temporal continuum. Even within Tenney's own compositional output, the existence of articulations is evident: the slight temporal variations in the tremolo *Koan* (1971) and the shifting spectral energy in *Having Never Written a Note for Percussion* are similar to the transitive harmonics and beating speeds in *Ajapajapam*. These articulations usually arise out of change within a single parameter; they don't form new temporal gestalts due to the low entropic nature of the change, but there *is* a perceived alteration within the sound. Importantly, in *Ajapajapam*, the singular form – the content of the piece – is not compromised, as the object remains as one large temporal gestalt, but the articulations are what maintain our active, performative listening throughout the piece, and what enables our auditory processing faculties to develop.

OVERCOMING FORM: REFLECTIONS ON IMMERSIVE LISTENING

Phill Niblock

Another sustained tone composer whose music describes simple formal shapes is Phill Niblock. The majority of Niblock's pieces are somewhere around the 20' mark, including all the pieces discussed in this section. The structures from a number of other Niblock's pieces involve a move either from divergence to convergence, or vice versa, employing very gradual linear glissandi (some pieces are more strictly linear than others), for instance the gradual convergence of *Five More String Quartets* (1993), and gradual divergence, for instance, *Sethwork* (2003), which ends with a mirrored convergence back to the unison from the beginning of the piece. A similar experience is provided to *Ajapajapam* in these pieces, in which an active, performative listening approach is capable of perceiving the surface articulations of transitory harmonics, beating patterns and combination tones, and exploring relationships between these. The global shape of the piece is comprehended not within a single present, as the movement is again too gradual, but by comparison throughout the piece. The different shapes employed by Niblock result in different experiential results: whereas in the case of a divergence pitch shape, the harmony expands outwards and more pitches are revealed to the listener, the convergent structure gradually reduces the harmony down to a single point, resulting in a distinctly different perceptual experience. The convergences in a piece such as *Five More String Quartets* provide an experience different to that of *Ajapajapam* in that, although this convergent point is the first time we hear unisons on their own, the clusters we have experienced throughout the piece have always bordered these unison frequencies, and they narrow very gradually – but in a completely linear manner – so that the close of the piece may be largely anticipated by the listener. In *Ajapajapam* there is no grouping around the final unison cluster until the very close of the piece. In *Five More String Quartets*, as we near the final point of convergence onto unison where tones are clustered so close together as to be within the critical band – and therefore cannot be parsed by even the most active of listeners – the surface beating patterns gradually slow down, reinforcing our sense of anticipation towards the unison. Interestingly, here it is the surface layer articulations that describe the final stages of the piece's shape for our perceptual processes; although the tones are still actually converging, we can only trace the shape through the beating tones. Form as content now takes on a significantly different meaning, wherein the foregrounded surface layer – described so far through this chapter as the primary object for a developed, performative listening – fuses with the background comprehension of the global shape, which we are now able to trace in real time (through the beating patterns) rather than just in retrospect. My own piece *Gradual Music* (2009) also reflects this experience, wherein the surface layer actually directs the pitch shape of the piece, due to the compact pitch clusters. The piece employs a structure of gradually expanding convergence-divergence shapes, before reaching a semitone cluster width, after which the structure reverses. These expanding and contracting clusters are perceived through the transforming beating patterns and help to guide the listener through the pitch shape of the piece.

To explore further the nature of the experience in Niblock's music, I will investigate the differences between *Disseminate* (1998), an orchestral piece, and *Valence* (2005) for viola played by Julia Eckhardt created within ProTools by multitracking pitch-shifted samples of the viola. Often Niblock's pieces are realised in a performance installation format, with performers placed throughout the space, so as to excite particular acoustics from the room. Whilst this is an important aspect of experiencing Niblock's music, the discussion of experience in an installation environment is left until the following chapter so as to allow this current chapter to explore shape and temporality in greater detail within concert and domestic listening environments.

Both *Disseminate* and *Valence* utilise sustained tones that gradually diverge from a unison into dense microtonal clusters, before converging back to unison. However, for all this similarity in approach to form, the construction and performative realisation of both pieces differs significantly. The importance of *ensemble* in *Disseminate*, as opposed to a solo player in the studio, is significant with regard to experiential differences. Although players are instructed to maintain stability on their own pitches within very tight microtonal clusters, they may well drift towards other pitches close by, therefore inducing further beating patterns and generating more perceptual articulations. The highly varying timbres in *Disseminate* result in a less homogenised global sound than in *Valence*, which is comprised solely of versions of the same sample, such that a high order of homogenisation would be expected. Again, the heterogenous orchestral sound of *Disseminate* results in the production of a greater number of auditory fluctuations, due to the combinations of the many varied instrumental spectra. This means that note entries and exits from the orchestral players – of which there are necessarily far more compared to the studio version of *Valence* – are more noticeable, despite the best efforts of the players, resulting in a multitude of actively-changing densities within the global sound.

Valence, which is also constructed using microtonal pitch clusters, sustains pure viola tones without the timbral differentiation of the orchestral piece. There are far fewer performed shifts in density as the tones extend without the kinds of indeterminate dynamic swells that occur when larger ensembles sustain tones; the listener therefore tends to be drawn towards the beating patterns within the sound, resulting in a vibrancy of dynamic articulations and the perception of a different type of transforming density. The potency of any articulations is magnified as there are fewer contrasting timbral factors towards which perception is drawn, and the stronger overall homogeneity means that our active listening is able to reach further inside the cluster of viola tones. Due to the sustained tone material, *Disseminate*'s diverse instrumental timbres fuse within our perceptions to some degree, but the many different performative techniques (both in terms of players' approaches, and the actions needed to generate tones from the assorted instrumental groups) ensures perceptual groupings occur from within the nature of orchestral playing as much as on the surface layer of the sound.

A performer in *Disseminate* is fully aware of how their current pitch relates to the overall global soundworld, due to immediate sonic feedback from the ensemble sound, and can balance their own tone accordingly. In contrast, the solo player recording extended tones in the studio hears only their own tone, and is able to focus in detail on maintaining a high level of consistency in timbre and pitch throughout its duration; there are no other simultaneously performed tones with which to interact, therefore sonic parameters retain a lower level of variance. The listener focuses more upon the finer articulations, but also becomes more cognisant of the overall divergence-convergence pitch shape of the piece as there are fewer, more overt transformations occurring with the clusters. This given, these smaller-scale articulations adopt a greater dominance within the global experience, and co-exist with comprehension of the larger-scale pitch shape.

These examples from Mažulis and Niblock show composers working with immersive sustained tone environments over relatively shorter durations who concern themselves with global pitch shapes that can be discerned throughout the piece. Another composer to whom this applies is Alvin Lucier, whose pieces *In Memoriam John Higgins* (1984), *In Memoriam Stuart Marshall* (1993), and *Charles Curtis* (2002), which each trace simple sine wave sweeps, are 20'06", 15'25" and 13'45"[2] respectively, indicating the shorter duration for perceiving these shapes. The orchestral pieces *Crossings* (1982) and *Slices* (2007), which also trace simple shapes, also last a shorter duration (16'06" and 19'00"). The concepts of these pieces – to demonstrate beating patterns at differing frequency points – demand certain kinds of shapes over others; however, in retaining the acoustic phenomena as clearly audible for the listener, Lucier projects a clear formal shape that can be experienced throughout the piece as a function of the beatings concept. The content demands the form.

---

2   *In Memoriam John Higgins*, *In Memoriam Stuart Marshall*, and *Charles Curtis* released on Alvin Lucier (ANTIOPIC ANSI002, 2005), *Crossings* released on Alvin Lucier: Crossings (Lovely Music LCD 1018, 1990), *Slices* duration specified at http://www.materialpress.com/lucier.htm.

OVERCOMING FORM: REFLECTIONS ON IMMERSIVE LISTENING

Eliane Radigue

Eliane Radigue is a composer of longer duration sustained tone music. Her work presents a somewhat different approach to creation and experience to that of Mažulis and Niblock. *Koume* is the third section of Radigue's *Trilogie de la Mort*, and was made in 1993; the *Trilogie* is inspired by the Tibetan Book of the Dead, and *Koume* is motivated in particular by the deaths of both her son soon after the completion of *Kyema* (the first *Trilogie* chapter), and her Buddhist master Nenang Pawo.

Koume is nearly twice as long in clock duration as *Ajapajapam*. It is a tape piece, and consists of very gradually shifting oscillator tones made using Radigue's ARP synthesiser. Upon listening to this piece, what I find is that the longer duration does not project a feeling of global shape as with the previous pieces in this chapter, but rather a much more reflective space for one's own personal inquiry. The nature of the piece is more about the changes we, as the listener, undergo, rather than what changes the material itself undergoes.

When making the piece, Radigue performs each strand of the global sound individually on the oscillator – each in one extended take – making pre-determined gradual changes on potentiometers (Kyle Gann uses the term 'glacial' to represent not just the speed but the awe-filled nature of the movement (Gann, n.d.)). In comparison to the performances on acoustic instruments in the Mažulis and Niblock, this electronic soundworld has less activity upon the surface layer in terms of fluctuations of beating patterns and transitory harmonics and overall density, as the continuity of each pitch is far more stable than even the viola in *Valence*. The beating patterns remain constant for longer as pitches remain fixed; our active listening has to expend more effort to retain memories of extended presents due to the lack of articulations. However, *Koume* never remains in a constant state for what feels like an overly-long duration, as another tone may gradually fade in, or a present tone fade out, resulting in a shifting articulation and prompting further surges from our outwardly-reaching perceptual processes.

The nature of this soundworld generates the more reflective state that Radigue herself acknowledges she is interested in creating. As she notes, '[t]he music acts as a mental mirror, reflecting the state of the receptive listener at the time' (Winship, 2010), and this state will likely transform throughout the piece's extended duration. Her sounds are intended to reflect something from the mind (Dax, 2012), and the constancy of electronic tones enables an achievement of this aim of an order higher than performers of acoustic instruments may be able, due to inevitable fluctuations in their sound that reflect the technique of performance and the performer themselves, rather than the listener.[3] This constancy of tone, and therefore surface phenomena such as beating patterns, contributes to a lessening of focus on a single, specific 'shape' that unifies the piece, and places emphasis upon the repetition of those patterns and the sustained nature of the tones at a given present moment.

For me, at a clock point similar to the full duration of *Ajapajapam*, I begin to comprehend, or actually *experience*, the entire scope of the whole work. It is clear that much of what I have heard already in the piece has prepared me for this enhanced experience of scale; it could not have occurred earlier in the piece, even with the same material. So, at some point, what had been termed 'form as content' in the case of Niblock and Mažulis, becomes 'form as scale'; the notion of shape has entirely dissolved, and been replaced by an expanded continuum. The previous material has not coalesced to generate a singular formal shape in which the present material can be placed, but rather, the material itself *expands*, projecting an image of a monumental scale. Clearly, there is no one universal durational point at which this occurs, but it is entirely dependent on materials used by the composer, the pacing over those materials over the duration, and the manner in which listening strategies have been adopted by the listener.

---

3 However, since 2001 Radigue has found great satisfaction in working with instrumental performers such as Charles Curtis, Kasper T. Toplitz, Carol Robinson, Bruno Martinez and Rhodri Davies. She has since stated that when working with the ARP synthesiser, 'every piece felt like a compromise between what I wanted to do and what I could achieve' (Wyse, 2011).

OVERCOMING FORM: REFLECTIONS ON IMMERSIVE LISTENING

In contrast to my descriptive approach above, Joanna Demers describes the listening experience of *Kyema* (the first piece of the *Trilogie*, but with a soundworld not dissimilar to *Koume*), in a discrete sectional manner, wherein separate blocks of texture are differentiated, and transform into one another at clear boundary points (2010, 94). To me, what seems to be missing in her account is the acknowledgement that, once we reach certain later stages of the piece, our listening approaches have been transformed, and we may not be assuming an analytical mode of listening that instinctively breaks the sound into discrete sections based on variance within sonic parameters. It is the extended duration that is the primary tool for engendering these transformations in our listening. The active, performative listening that we may adopt initially in the piece, and that we can maintain to some degree throughout *Ajapajapam*, *Valence* and *Disseminate*, transforms into a listening approach focussing upon the temporal field, as much as (if not more than) the current and past material. The music is comprehended as existing on such a vast scale that it seems easy to adopt the more reflective listening approach that Radigue discusses; it is not an acknowledgment of the global shape, in the manner possible with *Ajapajapam*; rather, it is an acknowledgement of the *breadth* of the piece. The immersive nature of the piece, in which continuity of material and duration overcomes surface layer articulations, prompts both expansion of comprehension of the sounding present, and an inward reflective state. Phenomenologist Thomas Clifton states that 'the identity of the present is established by what the past and future "see" of it' (1983, 57); I am able to grasp what the experience of the future of the piece will resemble (different to anticipating short-term upcoming material), which then – along with memories of experiences from what has already occurred in the piece – inform the knowledge and experience of what is occurring in the present. It is to experience the large-scale comprehension of the work itself.

However, once a transformation such as this has transpired, a single listening mode is not assumed over all others for the rest of the duration. Rather, the experience varies between and across these modes, wherein I am able to choose to listen actively to continuous beat patterns or densities, or *hear* them as a single continuum, or recede further and experience the scale of the piece, as a whole. In this sense, I remain active in following where my perception leads me; gradual transitions still occur within the material, and occasional articulations may reintegrate a more performative listening approach from one that focuses on scale. Likewise, the movement may become more and more gradual, so that I eventually cease to explore articulations and slowly transition into an approach exploring the expanded present, before transforming again due to the prompting of a higher activity in the perception of present material.

In an effort to explore this mode of listening further, I want to approach discussion negatively, by introducing a term that I feel does *not* describe my experience: 'timelessness'. For me, this is a term I tend to deliberately avoid in my writing, as it seems to curtail discussion, or put a barrier upon what could be further considered; in this music, I am experiencing temporality in some fashion, and it is my task to describe that to the best of my abilities. To explore the term further, we can turn to the work of analytic philosopher Robin Le Poidevin, who suggests that (away from discussing music specifically) when we describe something as 'timelessness', we might mean 'tenselessness': time without the flow of time. In relation to his work on John McTaggart's B-series, Le Poidevin explains that, whereas the A-series describes events that possess specific temporal properties of being either past, present or future, the B-series points to an underlying structure of events ordered by their unchanging relations to one another (before, simultaneous and after). Le Poidevin's 'tenselessness' derives from the distinction between tensed verbs employed for describing the A-series, to indicate whether an event is happening, say, in the future, and the 'tenseless' verbs used for the B-series, which do not point towards the 'flow' of time, or the individual's position on the timeline. Therefore timelessness, in this light, indicates the tenseless nature of the B-series: time without the flow of time. Le Poidevin states that what may be described as timelessness can be equated to a lack of past-present-future, in which we are left with events that 'be', rather than 'were', 'are' or 'will be' (Le Poidevin, 1990).

My issue is not with the above description, but rather with application of the term to the experience of music. Jonathan Kramer states that, despite its etymology, there is a 'time of timelessness', in which ordinary time has become frozen in an 'eternal now' (1988, 378); however, I see this receptive state, as described above, as an awareness of the larger scale of the piece, and a perception of the present through previous experiences of the piece, and through what experiences may transpire. It is an active state of perception and cognition, but of a different order to the performative listening described in the Niblock and Mažulis discussions. Timelessness – the time of timelessness – for me suggests too fixed and redundant an experience. I do not propose that this is an issue with semantics; whilst Kramer's time of timelessness, and my own listening approaches, describe similar areas, I see it as emerging from an active listening perceptual state, which gathers memories of experiences that then inform experience of the present; the music heard up until the present moment in the piece actively influences what, and how, listening occurs. I am a tensed listener, experiencing the music as I perceive it, with an evolved, adaptive listening approach.

In *Koume*, I don't experience a 'frozen time', but rather some sort of understanding of where I reside within the widened scope of this piece. The music does not *stop*, nor does my temporal experience; rather, my focus has been widened towards the scope of the piece, and how what I am listening to *now* fits within it. The primary material (the oscillator tones, whose sonic parameters continue to transform gradually) becomes the 'background', whilst the scope of the piece, the acknowledgement of a continuum, and one's temporal position within that, becomes the focus. This transformation of perception can only occur after some sort of extended duration, and within some kind of continuous auditory material – for which sustained tones are ideally suited. It is a transformation within the listener (rather than a transformation within the auditory material, which is continuous), who is then able to shift between these fluid temporal modes at will, deploying recollection and anticipation to the current sounding material to bring that back into the foreground. A simple analogy would be Pauline Oliveros's distinction between focal attention, which produces clear detail upon the object of attention, and global attention, which continually expands to include the whole of the space/time continuum of sound (2005, 13). Whilst what I am describing is quite different to Oliveros's deep listening, there is a sense in Radigue's music of shifting towards a comprehension of the entire scope of the piece, once duration takes hold.

Curtis notes that, by working with Radigue on her piece for solo cello, he learnt to hear as she hears (Curtis, n.d.), but I feel that there is a strong sensation of being guided towards this state by experiencing this music as well. Guided, rather than being told exactly what to listen to; patiently having expanses revealed within us. The nature of the submergence over the full duration begins to reveal a more comprehensive awareness of scale, and how material can create that scale. Perhaps we end up with form as content as scale; *Koume*'s sound continuum enables our listening to progress to a heightened awareness of overlap between material, duration and temporality as experienced. When writers bemoan a piece's extended duration (eg Clements, 2011), they ignore the constructive reasoning behind it; *Koume* demonstrates that the durational decision is as significant a part of the auditory experience as is the material, and it heavily informs the transformation into awareness of the scope of sound.

La Monte Young

To conclude this chapter, I want to discuss one of the most well-known sustained tone pieces, La Monte Young's *Compositions 1960 #7*. Middle B and F# are to be 'held for a long time', and Young notoriously demands that performances be played on continuously tunable instruments, and in no case on keyboards and synthesisers. The composer preferred to perform the piece in a concert setting, which places much more emphasis upon the fluctuations actualised by instrumental performance, however slight they may be, due to virtuoso performer technique. Whilst the listener tends to understand from the outset that there will be no structural change throughout the duration, they are prepared for transformations to occur within both the sonic result of the performance, and their perceptual processes and conscious awareness of the situation, as articulated within the discussion of *Koume* above. Our active, performative perceptual processes are able to extend outwards and 'touch' the various aspects of not only the auditory environment, but also the temporal flow as experienced, as we may choose to move the focus away from the surface fluctuations and towards what was the previously background continuum of the perfect fifth interval. Our temporal experience is in motion, a motion generated through our own perceptual processes. Clarinettist Anthony Burr has talked of the 'responsibility' being left with the audience to parse the overall experience (2012, 6), and this parsing can be applied to *Compositions 1960 #7* on a variety of orders: the two fundamental pitches can be experienced as an inseparable dyad sonority, or at the other extreme as separated pitches with a vast chasm of pitch space between them; the points of contact with standing waves, revealed through slight shifts in head position; the continuous flow of harmonic clusters arising from the two fundamentals, continuously shifting due to bow/breath pressure; and so on. This responsibility is quite separate from *Koume*'s reflective durational experience, or *Ajapajapam*'s comprehension of shape and surface articulation; whilst all of these may combine in the experience of *Compositions 1960 #7*, the fixed nature of the interval precludes gradual transformation. Articulations are still prevalent, but the anchored pitch continuum dominates my comprehension of the experience; it is not that I experience shape, as with *Ajapajapam*, but rather it is continuity, first and foremost, that drives my cognitive faculties. The experience is not of a duration, it is continuous; it maintains an inner momentum, a relentlessness of which it is our responsibility to process.

As Jeremy Grimshaw states, the concept is a raw statement upon notions of what music might be (2011, 49). Whereas Radige's *Koume* invites inward reflection of the individual through its oscillators' repetitive beating patterns, the perpetual dyad of *Compositions 1960 #7* is more of a declaration. However, this declaration has a pitch interval, which is performed by instrumentalists, with whom listeners develop a relationship throughout the duration of a performance. This relationship occurs within the enduring pitch continuum, and develops despite the fixity of actions performed. This continuous aspect of *Compositions 1960 #7* provides a link to the following discussion of experience in performed installations, which are as continuous and ever-lasting as the visiting listener wishes them to be.

© Mike Walker 2013

Performed installations

Richard Glover

This chapter follows on from the previous one, but does not restate its discussions of perception. I will further explore the issues of experiencing immersive environments within performed installations. These are taken to mean extended performances in which there is no division between performance space and listening space, in which performers are scattered throughout the installation space, and audience members (and occasionally performers) are able to move around and within, and may enter or exit at any time. I am discussing the experience of a fixed object that the listener understands clearly as simply having started, or been set in motion, at some point, as there is no formal development or transformation operating within the construction of the work.

The chapter derives very much from my own experiences of immersive sound installations, described in my own terms. I do not attempt to account comprehensively for the many different installation environments that operate over extended durations; rather, I am interested in exploring a single scenario in heightened detail. Similarly, the philosophy behind sound arts installation is not tackled here – this has been dealt with thoroughly elsewhere.[1] I discuss *performed* installations specifically because the concepts of the work (both the harmonic/timbral intent and the indeterminate fluctuations arising from performative issues) are realised through human agency, rather than through software performing pre-determined algorithms. In this way, I am able to involve discussion of the acts of performance, and the impact they have upon the listening experience.

---

1. See Voeglin, S. (2010) *Listening to Noise and Silence: Towards a Philosophy of Sound Art.* London: Continuum.

OVERCOMING FORM: REFLECTIONS ON IMMERSIVE LISTENING

The listening environment in which individuals are able to traverse the space in order to experience different listening locations promotes the notion of individuals taking charge of their own narrative throughout the duration of their stay. The very fact that listeners may enter and exit freely is a clear indication of this, and the varied locations of each audience member throughout the space, chosen according to their own set of subjective preferences, instils the notion of responsibility and performative listening. This occurs more strongly than in a concert environment (which need not necessarily entail a concert hall) in which people remain in a fixed position, and the intention is for all to experience the piece for its entire duration.

Canadian composer Chiyoko Szlavnics defines the level of engagement attainable with the surface of the sound in this work: '[m]y music requires that the listener step forward, come very close in order to see (hear) the details – just as one would in order to look at the details of the pigment on a painting' (2006, 39). Whilst this can clearly apply to the music of the previous chapter, it can be used to serve as a representation of the different acts involved within performed installation experience: a close listening to the details from an active listening mode, and physically moving towards a particular sound source to magnify further the nature of that sound. This ability to 'step forward' provides listeners with an opening to a great deal more complexity in their processing of a situation than when remaining stationary in one location. Alva Noë's perception-as-touch thesis manifests itself in both the physical and metaphysical worlds: audience members can reach out by increasing their proximity to sound sources, whilst they actively reach out with their own perceptual processes. Continuing the haptic framing, by physically reaching out with movement, the listener can determine how 'hard' perception touches auditory material by proximity and active listening, and how 'roughly' the auditory material is handled. The immersive installation experience is akin to archeology, exploring diffferent locations and occasionally finding something that resonates with yourself, and then seeing what can be found around or within it to contextualise, reveal how it is made, and perceive its finer details. It is an active role, in which continuous discoveries are made through the reaching out of physical movement and from a performative listening.

How might this affect durational experience? Consider James Tenney's *In a Large Open Space* from 1994, in which performers are distributed throughout the installation space and play long tones on a low fundamental and pitches from its harmonic spectra up to five octaves above. Due to the sustained tone material which is to be performed, duration as experienced in *In a Large Open Space* draws upon similar auditory processing as discussed in the previous chapter. However, as explained, the audience movement built into the piece renders this a different *kind* of perceptual environment – hence the need for a separate chapter.

In Tenney's piece, the performed harmonic spectra does not develop or transform into new sections. Pitches from the harmonic series are selected at will by individual performers, so that the global sonority is continuously and indeterminately shifting, and providing an immediate, comprehensible presence of the harmonic series in architectural space. The piece is, in keeping with Tenney's previous work, created as a single gestalt entity, whose inner details are exposed for closer inspection by the audience. Audience members are surrounded by individual performers continually renewing pitches, or switching to new pitches after a previous tone has been performed.

Robert Morris wrote about removing unnecessary internal relationships out of a sculpture so as to shift the focus to the space and to the viewers. His works could almost be seen as demonstration objects, which prompt an awareness in the observer of their perception of the associations between things and situations. In much the same way, Tenney has previously stated that he believed it was the function of art to explore reality through perception (Young, 1978, 4); he wanted his music to prompt a similar awareness in the listener to comprehend the magnitude of their listening capabilities, and the manner in which these can develop.

OVERCOMING FORM: REFLECTIONS ON IMMERSIVE LISTENING

There is a continuity within the experience of *In a Large Open Space*, somewhat different to that of Young's *Composition 1960 #7*, that arises from the constant sense of renewal of the soundworld. Tenney built in the instruction for the 12 or more performers of the work to avoid playing a partial that is already sounding, which gives the experience of the work a continuous movement; if instruments with diverse registral ranges are selected for the performance, then a good representation – if not the entirety – of the first 32 partials of the harmonic spectrum, as described by Tenney in the piece's instructions, will be sounded throughout the duration of the work. Tenney's instruction ensures that the performance will not sporadically narrow in upon only a few partials, which would suggest to the listener a hierarchical pitch structure at that moment. I am reminded of Chapter 7 of Cornelius Cardew's *The Great Learning*, which has singers choose new pitches independently – rather than choosing a note already being sung – if the only audible pitch is the one a singer has just sung. This ensures continuous transformation, rather than a narrowing in on one or two pitch centres.

We are in an age now where terms such as performers, hardware designers, coders and composers all slide into similar meanings. The listener becomes a part of that medley, as they create, perform, perceive, interpret, understand, question, re-create and so on.[2] Immersive sound environments like those under discussion provide platforms for individuals to expand and develop their perceptual capabilities, and thus fuel a curiosity and want for exploration. Pauline Oliveros is someone who states that her performing and composing come from her listening (Barry, 2013); her listening is the central driving impetus behind how she makes music.

In performed installations, the audience are not simply experiencing the space in relation to the sound sources; they are experiencing the space

---

[2] Indeed, in a performed installation such as this, the performers are very much listeners as much as the non-performers; however, to explore discussions of physical movement throughout the installation space, I will make a distinction between those listeners who perform in a fixed location throughout, and those who are able to move across the space freely.

in relation to the *performances* of those sound sources. Audience members engage with relationships between different performers, their sound sources and their placement within the lattice of all the sound sources. Michael Pisaro has written about the nature of the 'tangible presence of the performer when not playing ... whose singular presence is more important than anything written on the page' (2009). He is describing the solo instrumental situation, but I would extend it to include the performers sounding partials within the context of *In a Large Open Space*, in which the listener can choose to share a close, private, location with any performer, whose presence is magnified upon proximity.

The main aspect motivating each audience member in this format is the ability, and encouragement, to move around the space, upon their own terms. The reaching out towards auditory stimuli is then controllable via each audience member. Duration as experienced is related to the kinds of information received, which is controlled by physical movement. Movement decrees positionality to specific sound sources (termed 'instruments', whether they be mechanical, electronic, acoustic or other), clock durations at each position, and directionality of auditory perceptive apparatus (ears and head, and to a large degree, the body). The audience member performs their own interpretation of the installation, through movement – almost choreography – in response to their own perceptions reaching out towards the auditory material.

So, whilst we can perceive these sustained tone environments by processing the multi-layered detailed textures and associating the indeterminate nature of instrumental performance with resultant fluctuations, the movement allows a subsidiary layer of perceptual engagement, making possible a physical 'reaching out'. The listener then has a cause to move around, to reach out to further auditory textures.

Robert Morris explored how the viewer themselves can continually change the shape of an object by changing their own position relative to the work (1966, 234), and here it is clear how the sonorities of *In a Large Open Space* also change as the listener moves about the space, assessing transformations in density, spectral cohesion, dynamic consistency and other parameters. However, to further this idea in recognition of the performed nature of the installation, the work can be compared to the experience of a living sculpture, where one registers that perception of the sculpture will change not only if one changes location, but also that the sculpture will continually reorder itself of its own accord, and one's perception of one's location in relation to the sculpture will change with it.

My paths to different locations whilst experiencing *In a Large Open Space* clearly give me a significantly different temporal experience than if I had remained stationary during listening. Sometimes I settle in a location for a duration, before moving elsewhere and doing the same; this means that I will likely experience the *movement* between locations in a concentrated manner, and place more focus upon my active listening in each stationary location. I compare different locations, comprehending the surface activity of the sound in relation to the location of the players around me, their sound sources, and the acoustics of the room. This results in my experience overall being discontinuous, broken up into discrete sections at different listening locations in which I settle to perform active listening.

This is a different experience than if I decide to move continuously throughout an installation for an extended period of time, without an intent to arrive at a particular location – such that my movement is for itself, without a goal. Here, my concentration focuses more on my own interactions with the different locations of the performers within the space, and I listen to how my own movement directs my experience. I develop a much greater awareness of managing my experience: I learn how my distance from performers, or architectural features of the space, can affect timbral aspects of the sound, or surface phenomena articulations, or psychoacoustical processes within my perceptual system. As I move, the tempo of my walking becomes the most significant factor in my experience, and my own body takes on a much more compelling role in how I perceive my own location within the surrounding installation environment. My active listening incorporates my location and movement across the space in a manner that allows anticipation to play a larger role in shaping my experience. These factors heavily determine my awareness of temporality. When in transit, our focus becomes attuned to how our movement affects what we can hear, and how our active listening adapts to new, upcoming listening scenarios. Having reached a settled location, our active listening becomes more attuned to the present, and engages with comparisons with the past.

Likewise, when we settle in a location for an extended duration, we gradually become more aware of a heightened sense of scale, as the perpetual harmonic series extends lengthwise and we do not just consider what we have been experiencing for the duration of our stay already, but we also begin to anticipate the fixed harmonies far into the future. The *breadth* of the installation is made more apparent, as is our role of insignificant observer; the *temporal* field (within which I situate myself) extends outwards in both directions. However, when we move through various localised timbral and pitch fields to different locations, listening with a heightened awareness that informs our physical movements, the opposite seems to happen, and we are able to examine these different auditory fields and how our shifting perspectival view of them alters as we move through the installation space. Instead of the expanding sense of scale when we remain settled, there is a 'closing in' upon the sounds within our transforming auditory horizon, and we comprehend the piece at a confined, magnified level, rather than the extended level. Of course, many peoples' experiences of installations involve both transit across the installation space, and stillness in fixed locations for particular durations. Temporal experience is fluid and transforms as choices of how and where to experience the work are made. As these activities are combined, the listener develops a more detailed understanding of how their choices of actions within this specific sonic environment can constitute their experience.

I also find that the longer I stay in an installation, the more the modes of perception for remaining stationary, and moving, combine. Over what feels like an extended duration, my physical movement across an installation space becomes a repeated performance of movements I made earlier, and I draw upon recall to determine whether the sonic environment has transformed, and whether my own listening has developed, in a manner similar to that described in the previous chapter.

In consideration of our sensory awareness as we move around the installation, I want to bring in Don Ihde's notion of the perceptual auditory field, through which we develop a sense of the spatial periphery of our auditory sense. As I listen and move across the installation space I evolve a strong sense of my auditory perceptual field; it becomes a living field that transforms as I move, and I learn how the space of the installation affects its shape and scope.

Brandon LaBelle encapsulates what certain installation-creators have already suggested by describing the space of the installation 'not as static object, but as live instrument' (2006, 191). Spatiality becomes as an 'audible condition' that makes us aware of the nature of the installation space (2006, 192). The audience plays an active role in the experience of the artwork; responsibility lies with them, as they discover new aspects of the instrument and are free to perform it as they wish. David Farneth, in describing La Monte Young's *Dream House* of sustained sine tones articulating higher primes of a low fundamental, says much the same thing, stating that by tilting his head back and forth and from side to side, he felt as if he were 'playing the room like an instrument' (Farneth 1996). In both these examples, we can interpret 'room' and 'space' as the installation itself; the space is indivisible from the installation itself, not only housing it but also fulfilling the role of guide for the listener. Grimshaw suggests that the form for *Dream House* could be graphically represented as a map of the space, describing which sounds happen where (2011, 140). This is a powerful consideration, as the listener learns to control their own body and physicality to perceive these sounds, and to parse them against the background of many other phenomena occurring in that same location. Grimshaw talks about the 'supposedly static music' as hyperteleological, that is, goal-oriented, in that it prompted him to move to certain different locations (2011, 140); the sensation of space-as-instrument prompted him to feel that he must continue to perform in order to continue to experience the installation itself. This account describes an aspect of the immersive installation experience in which one is so prompted to explore the differentiated sonic materials presented throughout the space that physical movement from one location to another becomes not a simple choice of one among many, but instead a tracking of a singular line of enquiry to reveal something new about one's understanding of the situation. It is the same curiosity as was described in the previous chapter, but one in which the path is pre-determined, described by auditory events generated by human agents. For *In a Large Open Space*, these paths are necessarily different upon each realisation of the work due to differing performers, instruments, techniques and so on; it is directly apparent what generates these audible paths.

In terms of the installation space being perceived as altered through this transition into instrument, Robert Morris wrote that he intended for the large sculptures he created to alter the observer's perception of the total gallery space by their sheer presence (1966, 233). *In a Large Open Space* seeks to alter the space not just of the harmonic pitch field – such that we perceive a current combination of partials in the light of previous partials played that rest in our short term memories – and not just in the manner of LaBelle's spatiality as audible condition, but also the 'space' of each listener's temporal horizon. 'Spatiality' comes to mean a function of movement and duration, and as I move across the installation space, duration as experienced alters in a manner that wouldn't occur if I were stationary.

So, in this way, the active, performative listening described in the previous chapter is transformed into an active performance, stimulated by listening. Each audience member becomes a performer (to bring back the choreographer analogy), interpreting the intentions and soundworlds of the situation through their own physical, perceptual and cognitive actions. It is they who construct a unique experience upon each visit to the same installation, rather than specifically the instrumental performers. As I re-perform my movement and active listening across the installation space, I become more aware of the performers' actions as they play the partials of this harmonic series. I am able to recall experiences from when I traversed a particular path previously, and compare how both different pitches played, and the manner in which they are being played (variations in timbre, dynamics and so on made by the performers). As particular locations within the installation space prompt me to recall memories from earlier experiences, I find that I am better able to focus upon timbres from specific instruments.

Having discussed the nature of perception in relation to our auditory processes and bodily movement, I want to conclude with a consideration of how an audience member might reflect upon the form of *In a Large Open Space*. Upon experience, without the construction of the work known beforehand, after a certain duration it becomes clear that no directed formal transformation over a duration has been given to the actions of the performers, and that they will continue to play pitches from within a limited palette (although that palette may not yet be fully comprehended by the listener). There will be no new material introduced, the nature of the tones being performed will not alter, and the performance will consist of the finite combinations offered by the pitch choices (recalling Jonathan Kramer's vertical music, which 'defines its bounded sound-world early in its performance and stays within the limits it chooses' (1988, 55)).

What terminology, then, could we employ to discuss form in this context? Can a word such as 'form' apply to a piece such as this, with its continuity over duration entirely fixed, without development of any description? Perhaps the form is the harmonic series, in the lineage of Tenney's form-as-content; or perhaps it is the experience of a continually transforming audible image of the same, fixed harmonic series – due to the different durations of tones performed by the various individual instruments. Along with Grimshaw's proposals of a map-as-form, he describes the conceptually 'new' of the *Dream House* to be found not along the horizontal plane of time, but the vertical plane of space (2011, 138): perhaps the manner in which the sound disperses in the space can be a means to describe the form of a work. Or can we talk about 'form' in relation to the many listeners within a work such as this? And how to account for the fact that individual listeners remain within the installation for different durations, entering and exiting at different clock times?

Composer Liza Lim states that, over an extended duration, 'the idea of "form" is perhaps replaced by a complex of different experiences that one has during the event' (quoted in Saunders 2003, 8), and this shifting of the discussion towards the individual's involvement in the artwork proves a more relevant approach to exploring the subjective nature of immersive installations such as *In a Large Open Space* by allowing the different roles performed by the listener, through movement across the space of the installation towards specific locations, and the active, performative listening at various differentiated locations, to be the prominent factor informing one's relation with a performed installation. This renders irrelevant the fixity in construction, the varied experienced durations by different listeners, and lack of a pre-determined endpoint, as it points away from ascribing a formal descriptor to account for all experiences of the same installation piece. The performers, their articulations, these experiences through their choices of pitches, techniques, sonorities, all contribute to the subjective viewpoint. Form as experiences, or form *of* experiences, in which there is no universal form but rather one that cherishes the individual's own listening performance, ultimately satisfies Tenney's outlook on his own creative project: sound for the sake of perceptual insight (Young, 1978, 4).

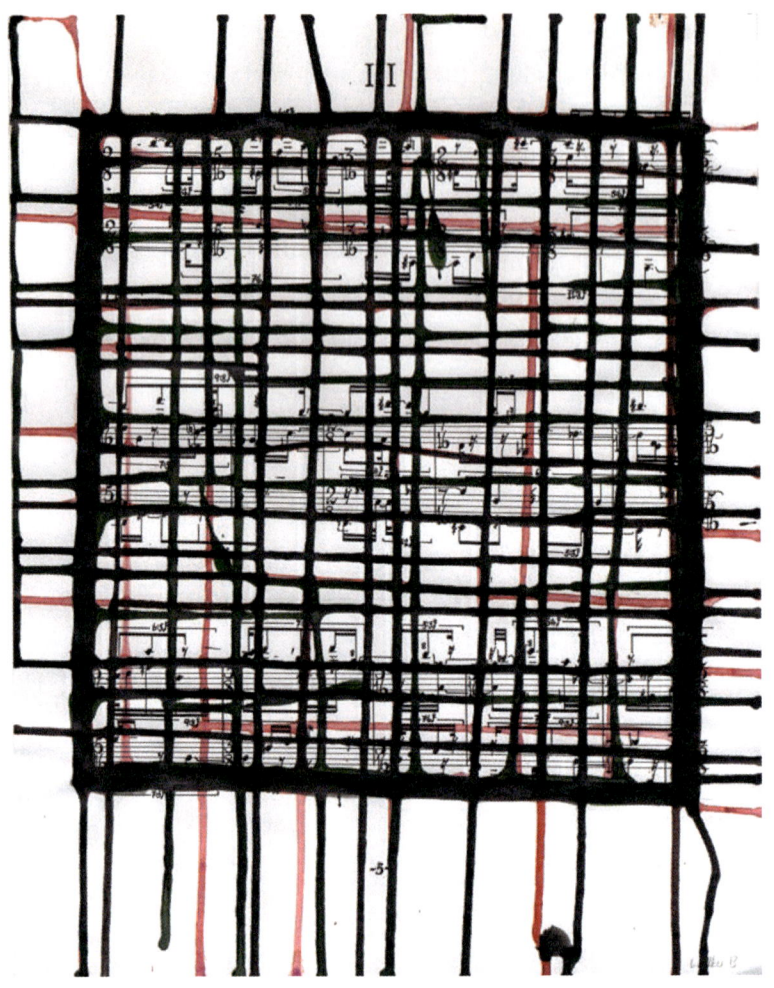

© Mike Walker 2013

Repetitions in extended time: recursive structures and musical temporality

Bryn Harrison

In an interview published in the *Ashgate Research Companion to Experimental Music*, Dutch composer Antoine Beuger discusses aspects of repetition and difference in his extended compositions. Astutely, he makes reference to an essay by Deleuze on the work of Beckett. Beuger asks the interviewer James Saunders:

> Do you know Deleuze's text about Beckett in which he differentiates exhaustion from fatigue? It's very inspiring. Exhaustion means all the possibilities have been explored, there are no more options left. Fatigue means one doesn't have the (physical) power to continue, even if the exploration hasn't come to an end. (quoted in Saunders 2009, 240)

The reference to Deleuze seems highly apt; Beuger's work, as Saunders suggests, similarly seeks to 'test structures many times to see what they might reveal' (2009, 240). In Beuger's works of extended duration, such as the *calme étendue* series (1996–97) (which can last between 45 and 540 minutes), each sound can be seen to take on its own autonomy, ultimately transcending its repetitious framework to appear as a 'world of singularities, of differences, of ultimate non-repetition' (2009, 240). In this chapter I will take a closer look at this subject by examining works that explore the full, exhaustive potentials of musical material through repetitious means. It would be no exaggeration to say that the focus of most of these works illustrate an almost obsessive sense of examining the same object over and over again, often from slightly different angles or perspectives. What I wish to advocate, quoting Hulme, is that 'repetition changes nothing in the object repeated, but does change something in the mind that contemplates it' (quoted in Deleuze 2004, 90).

OVERCOMING FORM: REFLECTIONS ON IMMERSIVE LISTENING

Although some of the works under discussion can last for several hours, this is not, as I will argue later, a prerequisite for a work that exhibits a large scale. Alongside the vastness of some of Beuger's piece and the late works of Morton Feldman, I will discuss works of a shorter duration by Kevin Volans and Howard Skempton. These works similarly appear to extend the perceptual timeframe by prolonging rather than varying their materials. It could be said that it is through this process of extension that we come to appreciate the immersive properties of the work. In examining pieces that exhibit a large scale through the repetition of smaller units, I will seek to demonstrate how these recursive structures can, as the British painter Bridget Riley has suggested (*Bridget Riley* 1979), act as an amplifier in giving significance to passing events. I will also consider the role of memory and question how near and exact repetition can operate in close proximity in providing points of orientation and disorientation for the listener (Harrison 2013). The essay will also draw on three of my own compositions and return in circuitous fashion to the work of Samuel Beckett where, I will argue, repetition not only plays an equally prominent role but to some extent serves a similar operative function to the musical counterparts I will discuss.

However, before discussing these works in more detail I begin with the perceptual challenges of listening itself. Maurice Merleau-Ponty, in his seminal text *Phenomenology of Perception*, tells us that 'consciousness constitutes time' (1962, 414). Merleau-Ponty states that 'we must understand time as the subject and the subject as time' (1962, 422). In other words, from a phenomenological point of view, time and being are inseparable; time cannot be intellectualised or understood in an empirical sense since this requires us to objectify time. As Merleau-Ponty reminds us, time cannot be 'seen' anymore than one can see one's own face (423–24). What he asks of us is 'to conceive the subject and time as communicating from within' (410). Much of the music that I find myself drawn to, and will discuss here, is that which seeks to position the listener at the centre of the work and through which meaning is acquired as an emergent property of the experience. The works that are being put forward here as examples are those that, I would suggest, construct time not from the 'outside' but from a more experiential standpoint that actively requires the participation of the receptive listener. What this music purports, I feel – as Merleau-Ponty would have us believe – is time as 'subjectivity itself' (422).

However, to place the listener at the centre of the experience, to allow her to bear witness to the present-centredness of the moment, requires a particular sensitivity to dealing with materials. Beuger's *calme étendue (spinoza)* (1997), with its intimate relationship between sound and silence, is such an example I feel. In its entirety the work consists of the successive reading of all the approximately 40,000 monosyllabic words from Spinoza's *Ethics*, painstakingly copied in their order of appearance. Each syllable is 'to be spoken in a very relaxed tempo (one word every eight seconds) and with a very quiet voice' (Beuger 2001).

The recorded version of the work I am listening to[1] begins with nine minutes of silence, followed by the narration of each monosyllabic word extracted from the Spinoza text, read by Beuger himself. Each event is carefully, clearly and quietly spoken and, as a listener, I am given time to reflect on each syllable as a sound (or as a combined inflexion) rather than as a word conveying its literal meaning. My attention is, at times, drawn to the endings of the sounds (the 's' of 'aus', or the 'ch' of 'durch', for instance) even though no change in pronunciation or emphasis occurs. Each syllable takes place within an eight-second timeframe that might seem highly periodic and yet is of a length that somehow makes it experientially difficult to measure. Each anticipation seems recharged from the last, creating a dynamic equilibrium between that that *is* (namely sound) and that that *is not* (namely silence); one might say that a pressure or force exists between words, akin to the surface tension on a still pool of water or the energy of a magnetic field.

---

1   Edition Wandelweiser Records EWR 0107 (2001).

After a period of several minutes, a substantially longer silence occurs again. Despite having listened to the extended silence at the start of the work, the absence of the spoken word appears unexpected at first, as if the spoken word is about to make itself audible again but has perhaps, somehow been pushed back in time. Eventually I accept the longer silence that ensues and a vista opens; the work transforms momentarily from a hermetically concealed world to an inclusive, open environment. However, for me, this opening horizon does not provide a place of refuge – it is not merely a space between events but, conversely, an attentive silence that is pregnant with anticipation since there is the strong suggestion that the alternation of syllable, silence, syllable, silence will once more return.

Several minutes later the alternation of sounds and short silences at regular eight second intervals resumes and my feeling is of being carried along on a thermal. Like air drifts, this sense of motion feels as if it is conveyed through something immeasurable; invisible to the eye and yet highly palpable. This eventually seems to give way to what feels like a sense of both sounds and silences becoming omnipresent, despite no actual change having occurred within the alternation of events themselves; I am in both a sounding and a silent space. This is broken by a small but significant occurrence – the incidental repetition of the same syllable through which one is reminded of the role of memory and also of the fact that these syllables are in fact excavations from a buried Spinoza text; these are words that had their origins in a grammatology, held in place through syntactical relationships and that have made a chance occurrence into the 'real world'.

As I continue to listen, the longer silences gain more structural significance. These silences seem spatial; I feel as if I am 'inside' the piece, it seems to be in front of me, behind me, perhaps akin to Merleau-Ponty's 'field of presence' (1962, 415). These a-periodic silences can feel long, but how long? One must wait, attentively; these are not pauses or moments of inactivity but moments in which silence feels immanently present.

Through this alternating structure of sounds that occur every eight seconds and much longer silences, one finds that there almost appears to be two dialectics at play in this work. On the one hand there are the relationships between one sound and the next, and on the other, the relationships between each sound and the short silences that precedes it. As Peter Ablinger has suggested with regard to Beuger's work, it can feel like the silences are the materials of the piece through which the sound events act as pauses or momentary interruptions.[2] This sense that the hierarchy between sound and silence has seemingly been reversed is highly significant to our sense of time perception in the work, since it suggests something closer to an immeasurable open expanse onto which the periodic events are placed.

Jürg Frey, a Swiss composer closely associated with Beuger and the Wandelweiser group, makes the interesting claim that there is a perceptual form of listening that exists between a more historically-positioned narrative time and time as an open expanse (Frey 2004). In discussing his own music he says: 'I am on the precise threshold where static sonic thinking almost imperceptibly acquires direction, where static, wholly motionless sounds meet the onset of movement and directionality of the sound material' (Frey 2004). What might the 'directionality of the sounding material' be in Beuger's work if the only 'materials' are those of spoken utterances? Perhaps it is that the sounds are successive – we wait in anticipation for the next sound, threatened only by the imminent arrival of a longer pause or the eventual cessation of the work altogether.

This threshold between motion and stasis that Frey speaks of might operate in other ways. In the late works of Morton Feldman for instance, temporal ambiguity is created through the reiteration of self-similar motifs, often within altered or differing contexts. As Dora A. Hanninen has stated:

---

[2] Conversation between Bryn Harrison and Peter Ablinger, 12 March 2013.

> Feldman's late works are characterised by patterns that acquire temporal extension through repetition. Significantly, in late Feldman pattern extension tends to involve not literal extension but semblances of repetition – numerous, often uncoordinated, adjustments in duration, timbre, and pitch. Feldman's penchant for pattern extension by near repetition poses a distinct cognitive challenge: the proliferation of near repetitions frustrates attempts to prioritise events by distinctive features, and thereby to categorise, or even remember, individual instances. The result is a superabundance of nuance that eludes conceptualization, leaves listeners with little to report, analysts with little to say. (2004, 227)

Feldman himself has talked of 'a conscious attempt at '"formalizing" a disorientation of memory' (2000, 137), in which he would 'have the same thing come back again, but…just add one note' (quoted in Deforce 2008). This perceptual game, I would suggest, serves to reinforce the intimacy of the work, placing emphasis on the smallest of events despite the considerable length of the overall work. As Feldman has said, 'Scale is no barrier to an intimate art' (quoted in Villars 2006, 80). However, the ways in which this intimacy is created tends to vary according to the works. Below I consider two different examples from Feldman's late period: *String Quartet II* (1983), which presents a relatively large number of contrasting materials over a highly extended period of time (in some versions up to six hours) and the orchestral work *For Samuel Beckett* (1987), which, by contrast, can be considered 'monolithic' in its outlook (Paccione 2010) through the ways in which the composer extends a singular temporal module over the course of approximately 55 minutes.

One of Feldman's guiding principles was to work intuitively, which is not to say that no process was used, but rather to suggest that he may, at any point, have broken off into something else. Feldman's longest work, *String Quartet II* offers an extreme version of this approach through which the listener is required to make continual adjustments to their listening as each momentary structure – sometimes of only a few unrepeated bars or sometimes, by extension, of up to several minutes – gives way to another. Magnus Olsen Majmon notes that:

> A first reading of the score causes a vague feeling of an enormous number of differentiated structures or fields with a repetitive character. A more profound analysis though reveals a work containing a relatively large, but comprehensible number of fields of differentiated character.' (2005, 4)

Majmon distinguishes three different field-categories: motifs, chords and patterns. From a purely analytical perspective, Majmon's categorisation is useful and one can easily work up a chart illustrating how the various types of materials recur through the piece, at what proximity and how many times. What this might provide for the analyst is a kind of visual map, a birds-eye view of the work, seen in an instant. However, the perceptual reality – the identity of the piece in which Feldman was most interested – is quite different. What makes the work truly profound for me are the ways in which Feldman makes the experiential aspect of the work render this comprehensible number of fields perceptually impossible. Previously heard events may be repeated exactly but most often contain some slight variation which may or may not be identifiable perceptually without the aid of the score or multiple hearings. These events sometimes occur in relatively close proximity (ie placed on either side of another segment which may, in itself, have been heard previously) or rendered audible again after a period of over an hour. Some events become accumulative and appear almost as themes, whilst others appear only once. (For an experiential account of such an approach, see the final chapter of this book.)

This perceptual terrain is made more complicated by several other factors such as: (i) the material or gestural content of some events being registered more significantly within the memory than others; (ii) the majority of passages being subjected to high but differing levels of repetition (often presented as slight variations of repetitions already heard); (iii) the relative degrees of self-similarity within the materials themselves (ie an abundance of class 1 and 2 intervals) making the job of discerning one discreet event from another all the more difficult; (iv) the temporal ordering itself through which the characteristics of a segment may be altered through context; and (v) the long duration of the work, which inevitably makes concentration itself an issue.

Yet none of the above can really account for the sheer visceral presence of the material itself. Feldman, it would seem, has the uncanny knack of keeping us alive to the moment. The constant interplay of a four-note pattern, the reiteration of a chord sequence with sudden shifts of dynamics or the seemingly melancholic playing out of a repeated theme against a suspended chord keeps our attention focused on the unfolding of events as they occur. It is not that we find recalling past events difficult but rather that, caught up in the moment, we do not spend the majority of the time concerning ourselves with the act of recall at all. We are only asked to bear witness to a past once it is already manifest in the present moment and then, whilst we try to relate this to the present situation, it has passed, becoming only a memory of a past event.

Through this process – this presence with a trace of the past – we become lost because of the difficulty of remembering. We are forced to resign ourselves to whatever happens next. Like Beuger's *calme étendue (spinoza)*, we submit to the moment. What we bear witness to in Feldman's work is what I have termed a kind of 'diary form'. As with diary entries, some are long, some are short, some are eventful, and others are less so. At times, pages of entirely new material rub up against each other, often contrasting, refreshing and extreme. At other times, the material seems to take on a kind of 'anonymity' (to borrow Feldman's term) in which it seems almost neutral or repetitive to the point of rendering the piece less 'visible'. Each 'entry' is penned in ink by hand and remains uncorrected. There is no editing to the score, no going back over things – they stand as an imprint of a moment in time. As Feldman explains, 'You have to have control of the piece – it requires a heightened kind of concentration. Before, my pieces were like objects, now they're like evolving things' (quoted in Rockwell 1999).

Through this constant act of repetition, contrast and renewal, an understanding of part-to-whole relationships within the work becomes redundant. Indeed, the fact that the internal elements are not proportional to one another becomes meaningless. The edges of the canvas, so to speak, are out of sight and the work is viewed as one immersive experience. Musicologist Bob Gilmore has described such an approach as 'overcoming form', stating that, 'in this exploded time-space, questions of form became essentially irrelevant' (2006).

It might be considered that what Feldman offers to the listener instead is a much closer (one might say magnified) perspective of the materials through which we are invited to focus on the subtlest aspects of change. It is not that we peer over the vast chasm presented and see the largeness of the work before us; instead we bear witness to the continual occurrence of small localised events through time. Feldman, I would argue, is not the heroic composer of works of grand proportions but a miniaturist, creating intimate works that often last several hours. Feldman says something similar with regard to the piece *For John Cage* (1982) 'It's a little piece for piano and violin but it doesn't quit' (quoted in Villars 2006, 131). Feldman is aware of the limitations of memory and the perceptual ambiguities that will ensue. In conversation with Michael Whiticker about *String Quartet II*, Feldman says, 'I think that the piece is so long because our attention span is so short' (quoted in Villars 2006, 185). It might be said that, as our memories fail us, we lose sight of the larger picture and resolutely focus on the small things. Feldman's success is our failure to comprehend the bigger picture. Faced with the disparity of not really knowing where we are in the work or where we are going simply adds to the abstractness or intangibility of the experience.

Dora A. Hanninen perceptively draws upon the emergent qualities that arise from such an experience. Hanninen uses the notion of emergence to highlight the difficulties of applying traditional analysis to these late works.

OVERCOMING FORM: REFLECTIONS ON IMMERSIVE LISTENING

What she stresses is that it is the accumulative aspect which gives meaning to the work and that, being experiential, is not something that can be demonstrated logically by examining the sequential ordering of events (2004, 232). This notion of emergence is particularly pertinent to the chamber orchestra work *For Samuel Beckett* (1987). In contrast to the highly segmented *String Quartet II*, what we bear witness to in the orchestral work is the temporal unfolding of one large texture. The immersive quality of the work and its vast sense of scale is something felt, not measured. A proliferation of dyads within the different instrumental groupings produce a hazy interplay of harmonic fields that continually cross like plates of glass placed on top of one other. The harmony is dense, ambiguous and occupies a large range of the spectral field. Any, feeling of it being functionally or teleologically conceived is replaced by slight durational distinctions and changes in orchestration that causes the composite elements of the harmonies to overlap in continually changing ways. Working with a reduced musical pallet, Feldman draws our attention to what is there, keeping us attentive to the subtle nuances of the piece. We may learn to appreciate how what at first may have seemed flat or forbearing is in fact imbued with depth through which registration, timbre and tessitura become elements to behold.

Over time, we start to search the temporal space, looking for relationships between chords or perhaps to the subtle patterning interplay between the harp, piano and vibraphone. Now, as I listen to the piece, I witness the subtlest of interplays between the various pitch ranges. Signifiers such as the different rhythmic placements between the various sections of the chamber orchestra, the particular tessitura of an instrument or the slightest pauses between entries, become more and more pronounced. I am perhaps twenty minutes in and am aware that the pitch patterns that comprise the continual chiming of the harp, piano and vibraphone have inevitably changed but I cannot say how. The interplay between woodwind, brass and strings seems slower and more spacious. Could this simply be the auditory effect of prolonged listening?

What I am hearing is a constant translation of the same pitches, the continual re-orchestration of the same materials. The dedication to Beckett seems apt; Feldman has spoken of how Beckett would write in English, translate into French and then back into English again. After receiving the text for the opera *Neither* (1977), Feldman spoke of how he at first found the text incomprehensible and then realised that what Beckett was saying was the same thing over and over again in nuanced ways (quoted in Villars 2006, 194). To return to the Deleuze quotation, there would appear to be the same difference here between exhaustion and fatigue. As I reach the end of *For Samuel Beckett* I get a sense that, like reading Beckett, all the possibilities have been exhausted through a continual search. The end of the work is not the point at which the materials have become over-tired or outworn, but the point at which renewal seems futile.

As was noted in the introduction to this chapter, the process of extension to create works that yield a greater sense of scale is not exclusively the domain of works that are governed by long durational spans. It is for that reason that other works such as Howard Skempton's string quartet *Tendrils* (2004) (20') and Kevin Volans's work for two pianos *Cicada* (1994) (25') might be regarded as exhibiting a large scale despite their comparatively shorter duration. In both of these works the part-to-whole relationships are severely reduced, resulting in work that, for me, seems longer in terms of clock time than what has actually passed.

In Skempton's piece, we bear witness to the continual modulation of 55 canons over a span of some 20 minutes. The material is linearly conceived and modal in content, which gives the impression of a harmonic texture that stretches out in time without recourse to any kind of teleological development. The effect is somewhat like what Jonathan Kramer would have referred to as a 'non-directed linearity', in which a sense of movement is pervasive but at the exclusion of an end-point or goal (Kramer 1988, 61–62). The emergence of melodic lines that seem to arise perpetually from each previous one can be attributed to each modal entry being a minor sixth above the previous one, creating the impression, through time, of a piece that is inwardly but continuously mobile. There are small resolutions within the music, but these become once more a point of departure. The impact upon the scale of the work is felt relatively early on. The anticipation of some kind of melodic development occurring within the work is quickly replaced by the sense of a continuum – of a textural interplay, of continuous counterpoint between the four parts of the string quartet. As I listen, now mid-way through Skempton's work, I am aware of an experiential shift. Initially it was the canonic entries that seemed foregrounded, but my attention is now drawn to the countermelodies that Skempton playfully weaves around the continually rising and falling canons. By the end of the work I feel as if my mode of listening has changed considerably but that the music has not really gone anywhere. Again, the transformative experience would seem to come from within rather than from the ways in which the music asserts itself upon us as listeners.

The interlocking of chords in Volans's *Cicada* for two pianos produces an alteration of dense harmonies that are, for the most part, subject to high levels of repetition. The materials are presented in panels of slightly contrasting length, each of which is preceded by a pause. With the exception of panels that are performed as singular events, these are repeated then replaced in turn by another panel that can be heard as a variation on the one that preceded it. The result is a series of windows onto an array of subtly shifting harmonic patterns. As Adrian Smith has said:

> Volans ... seeks to exploit a totally unpredictable shifting in the listener's perceptions. The object in the music, a repeated interlocking pattern, is not subjected to a fixed procedure but instead assumes the role of a highly malleable entity so that its status is continually in a state of flux. (Smith, 2011)

Perhaps unsurprisingly, Volans cites a visual source as the stimulus for the piece, namely the light sculptures of American minimal artist James Turrell. The similarity is clear; as with viewing one of Turrell's *Skyspaces* (Smith, 2011) the composer's intention is to draw us into a space for reflection or contemplation, where change is observed gradually and minimally. Smith perceptively describes the emergence of 'inherent rhythms' within the overall perceptual field, which he describes as 'patterns which are not directly played by the performer but which emerge out of the total complex of the music' (2011). As Smith notes, clearly perceptible streams of quavers form in the top voices of each hand whereby notes are not perceived separately but rather as the result of a gestalt sensation (2011). Volans additionally makes slight shifts in tempo and nuanced variation in the dynamic interplay between chords to emphasise these differences. Repetition here serves the function of providing temporal extension, which, in turn, highlights the inherent characteristics of each particular panel.

Finally, I wish to consider issues of temporality and, in particular, the role of repetition in my own works. Dealing with notions of time has been a guiding principle in much of my music since 1995 and has directly affected my approach to structure and the ways in which materials are utilised. Repetition has been integral to this way of thinking, particularly as a device for placing an emphasis upon the experiential aspect of the work. I will focus in particular on three pieces of differing duration – *Surface Forms (repeating)* (2009) (10'30"), *repetitions in extended time* (2008) (45') and *Vessels* (2012/13) (76') – that examine highly recursive structures over differing time scales.

The experiential disparity between a relatively short durational span and a large scale outlined in the Skempton and Volans pieces above is also explored in my composition *Surface Forms (repeating)* scored for an ensemble of eight players plus soprano voice and tape. Despite the relatively short duration of the work, the high level of textural density, coupled with the seemingly endless self-similarity inherent within the material itself, produces a single block of sound. As I have stated elsewhere, what we hear are:

...fluttering, ephemeral surfaces that quietly but actively engages the listener in the passing of fleeting events. Successions of notes that operate at a speed beyond that which can be immediately apprehended are repeated again and again, allowing the listener to gradually build up an understanding of the composite elements of the textural surface over an extended period of time. (Harrison 2013).

The pitches are derived from a series of interlocking descending chromatic canons that repeat over and over throughout the piece. These canons are then organised into a metric framework that operates on cycles of 43 seconds. With the return of the cycle, materials may be repeated, altered or replaced with new material.

Whilst preparing this chapter, I am listening to the recording of the piece afresh and am reminded that the textural surface appears so saturated at first that it seems almost impenetrable. Pianist Philip Thomas described the experience to me as rather like climbing a rock face of which we cannot quite get a grasp.[3] The soprano voice, intoning single syllables, is foregrounded against a bristling backdrop of activity provided by the ensemble. The quiet yet unrelenting surface does not let up – the persistence of the material and the sheer speed and density of the texture provides a kind of continuum through which we witness a tangle of interweaving lines. I am similarly reminded of hearing the piece for the first time during rehearsal with the ELISION ensemble. I remember feeling decisively 'outside' the music for the first few minutes, unable to get a foothold on the events that were quickly passing by. As I continued to listen, my relationship with the surface of the work changed. The voice became less foregrounded and I began to sense direct repetitions embedded within the fabric of the texture. As I listen to the piece now, a descending clarinet motif, identifiable earlier in the piece, is heard again. Am I revisiting the same point in the music or is this motif now heard against a

---

3 Conversation between Bryn Harrison and Philip Thomas, 27 August 2013.

different backdrop of changing motifs? Of course, having written the piece, I have perhaps a better understanding from a perceptual perspective, but I am nevertheless surprised how little I feel I recognise within this surface texture. There are, very literally, pages of material that repeat in exactly the same way and yet I rarely hear them as such. The surface is simply too dense and the cycles too long for me to recognise every aspect of the repeated page.

After the work's first performance at the 2009 Huddersfield Contemporary Music Festival, composer Pat Allison perceptively remarked to me that the listening experience for him had been somewhat like skip-reading through a book.[4] If this imaginary book hypothetically contained exact duplications of pages we would not necessarily recognise them as such since we would most likely be reading a different point on the page. Of course, having heard the piece many times, I now know the piece considerably better – although its inner-complexity still perplexes me. It would seem our memories allow us to recall some of the details of past events but prove insufficient in providing enough of the details to make the experience entirely quantifiable, even if the events taking place are in relatively close proximity.

By contrast, *repetitions in extended time*, as the title suggests, is conceived over a larger time scale (45'). The music is presented in five closely-related and inter-connected discreet panels, which offer different perspectival views on similar materials. Each panel is played at a slower speed than the last, whilst the degrees of repetitions become progressively greater from one panel to the next. As with *Surface Forms (repeating)*, at first the fleeting passing of events makes the music seem almost out of grasp. As I listen, three distinct layers skirt around each other: streams of constant demisemiquavers in the piano part are pitted against the rhythmic irregularity of the bass clarinet and electric guitar, and freer, oscillating glissandos in the string parts. Against these layers can be felt the pulsating regularity of dense chords played by two

---

4 Conversation with composer Pat Allison, Huddersfield Contemporary Music Festival, 26 November 2009.

electric keyboards. Because each panel consists of groupings of instrumental parts that are given their own number of repetitions, what I hear is a latticed textural surface of interlacing loops and circles. The surface, as I listen, appears multi-perspectival, each layer timbrally and rhythmically distinct enough for us to shift our gaze. As the piece moves into the next panel, the texture now transforms into a rhythmic interplay between the clarinet, electric guitar and strings. I become aware of slight alterations in rhythmic placement, crossings and shifting patterns. The rhythmic consistency of the endless streams of demisemiquavers in the piano part can now be perceived as a grid of sorts, an anchor point that helps to highlight the persistent irregularity of the rhythms in the clarinet, electric guitar and string parts.

As the piece progresses I become gradually aware of a reduction in tempo and a spatial dimension emerges. One does not relax but is, perhaps, allowed to ease into the music, the motion becoming more bodily (perhaps akin to breathing). The repetitions increase but I have had time to adjust, to become more immersed in the fabric of the music. Over time the piece becomes more singular, slower and more obsessively repetitious. As I listen to the final panel, the music feels as if it is taking place in slow motion, suspended in time, no longer fleeting. *repetitions in extended time*, as I see it, is very much about taking the listener to the heart of a sound, magnifying events – creating the embodiment of a living, breathing experiential time. In other words, it *requires time* to in order to become embodied by *time itself*.

Of the three pieces of mine under discussion, the encapsulation of a single musical moment extended out over a prolonged time scale is most acutely experienced in my solo piano work *Vessels*. At over 76 minutes, this work stands as my longest solo work to date. There are no distinct sections, no development of material, no changes of dynamic, just an ongoing impetus of expanding and contracting pitch intervals within a confined registral range; a magnified picture of a self-similar whole. Inspired by the pitch processes used by Skempton in *Tendrils*, all the material for the piece is similarly constructed from a nine-note Messiaen mode which, as in *Tendrils*, is subjected to its various transpositions. Unlike Skempton's piece, however (in which the material is linearly conceived as a series of canons), *Vessels* presents simultaneously rising and falling contingent pitches from the mode, which are continually altered registrally through octave transposition. A single cycle of the pitches is encapsulated within just the opening bar of the piece and, in effect, all subsequent bars can be seen as slight modulations and variations of this brief cyclical process. High degrees of repetition of either single bars, groups of bars, or whole pages offer slightly differing perspectival viewpoints on the material.

When listening to the first few minutes of the work I find myself aware of the constant regeneration of pitch patterns, sometimes transposed to related harmonic areas. Repetition appears rife but seemingly never exact. Pitches seem to be constructed from arcs that momentarily cross, appearing almost as small cadential figures that never quite resolve; their point of arrival becomes only a point of departure. The constant near repetition of pitch and rhythm becomes quickly disorientating; a process is discernible but the perceptibility (or perhaps predictability) of the process is intentionally kept slightly out of reach – there are enough possibilities within the process to keep the music in a constant state of flux. As the piece continues, one begins to sense that the music is essentially one tiny moment, examined hundreds of times – a single event stretched out over 76 minutes.

A comparison might be made here with much of Feldman's late music (see my own observations on listening to Feldman's *Triadic Memories* given in Chapter 5), in which register begins to assume more importance over time. Notes in the highest and lowest registers often appear to gain in significance, becoming transitory points of focus. As I listen to *Vessels*, I find this is particularly noticeable in passages subjected to particularly high levels of repetition (a three-bar passage repeated seven times for instance), where one is able to dwell on these small events for longer. Similarly, nuanced variations in rhythm acquire greater prominence through reiteration. Extension through the repetition of single units becomes especially significant from a point one third of the way into the work where the first 11 pages are repeated and form what would appear from examining the score to be an A/A structure. However, a key difference is that additional repetitions are added or the number of repetitions changed in the repeated pages. For the most part the number of repetitions is considerably increased, which has the affect of more than tripling the length of the piece.

As with *Surface Forms (repeating)* the literal repetitions of pages are difficult to discern, due to the continual iterations of small localised recursive structures and the high degree of self-similarity within the material itself. In *Vessels*, these differences are felt more acutely due to the varying degrees of extension through repetition. We can perhaps no longer say that these are the same pages since their identity has been changed. As I write, I am listening to a passage some 50 minutes into the piece. The rhythms are uncharacteristically regular within the context of a work that consists largely of slight deviations in rhythmic proximity. The regularity becomes more persistent by virtue of the high levels of repetition given to the passage. Although the material is a repetition of the same passage presented earlier in the work, its characterisation is transformed into something that sounds new. I feel it is interesting to note that, for the CD of the work, Philip Thomas (to whom the piece is written and dedicated) wished to record the piece in a single take with no further edits. Thomas is intrinsically aware that things change through time, that the subtlest of changes to the way a passage is played will have some performative effect on what immediately follows and that the experiential aspect of time itself will have a significant impact upon how the piece is performed.

An interesting parallel to this work can be seen in Samuel Beckett's short prose work *Lessness* (English edition 1970). Steven Paton has described how the *Lessness* uses formal means such as 'exceptionally high levels of repetition and parallelism' (2009, 357) to remove a sense of narrative progression from the work. Like *Vessels*, the second half of *Lessness* can be seen as a repeat of the first. The text consists of 60 sentences, which are then randomly reordered and through which 'the forces of successivity – movement in time and narrative progression – [are] replaced by a radical simultaneity in the text' (2009, 357). The 'timelessness' to which Beckett's title alludes is inherent within the construction of the work; there is no sense of progress and no sense of 'getting anywhere'. As we read on into the second half of the text we are not directly aware that the sentences are repetitions of the first half as there is nothing to imply a sequence, just a constant set of iterations. As with the aforementioned musical examples there is a feeling of ambiguity to the part-to-whole relations that has a significant bearing on our overall perception of the work. Deleuze's description of exhaustion in Beckett's work is beautifully played out here; Beckett does not stop until every line has been repeated, until every possibility has been exhausted.

Whilst I will resist drawing any immediate conclusions from what has been discussed in this chapter it remains to be said that each of the examples chosen for discussion demonstrates a remarkable propensity for making 'time itself' the subject of the work and through which the immediacy of the moment manifests itself as a living, breathing entity. Kramer makes the crucial point that the present is not simply the place where perception happens but 'it is also the meeting ground of memory and anticipation, both of which colour perception' (1962, 367). In other words we find ourselves living both in and through time, constantly engaging with our faculties of memory protention and retention. Time can be seen as both the instant and the accumulation of instants that make up the 'being-time' that we experience. This sensory accumulation of musical events both immediate and more distant, this moment and perhaps the imminent suggestion of what is to come, create an interweaving presence that is both reassuring in its sensorial actuality yet disconcerting in its absence – as soon as I try to give it a name and a place it is gone.

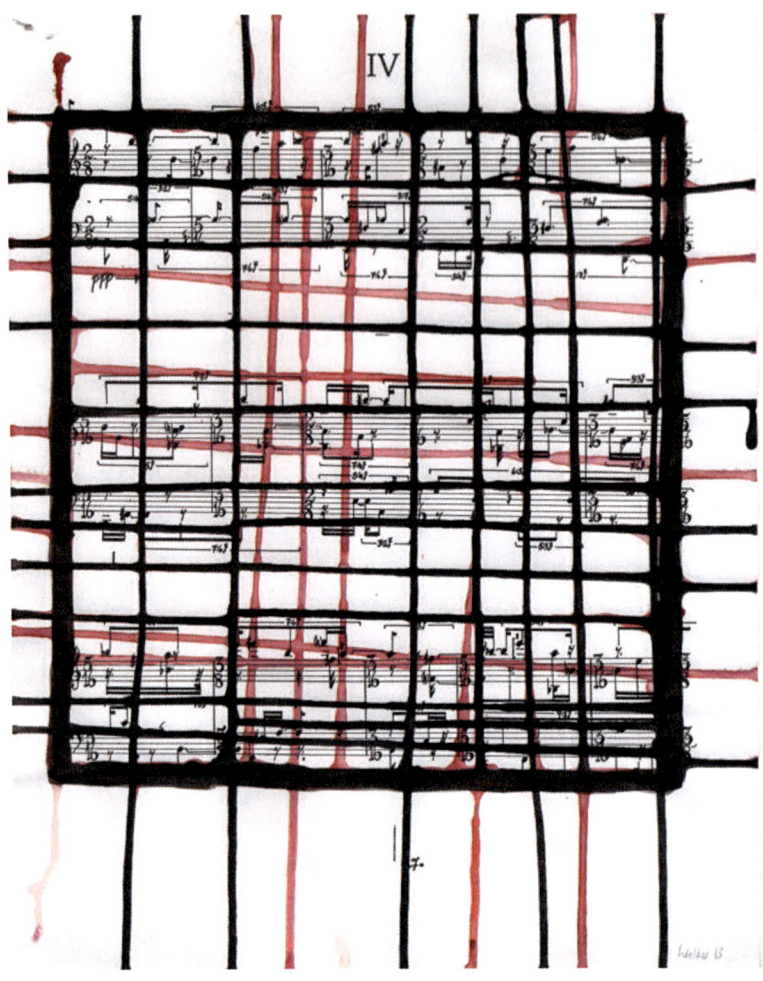

© Mike Walker 2013

Listening through Morton Feldman's *Triadic Memories*

Bryn Harrison

What follows are my own personal reflections on Morton Feldman's 1981 extended solo piano composition Triadic Memories. *The text is based on the 17 pages of notes that I made in the early hours of 16th August 2013 whilst reflecting closely on Aki Takahashi's performance of the work (ALM Records – ALCD-33, 1989) through headphones. There are several other recorded versions that I could have used, such as those by Louis Goldstein, Roger Woodward and the two editions of Jean-Luc Fafchamps. As with other extended late works by Feldman slight variations in tempo can lead to recordings that vary considerably in length. At just over an hour, Takahashi's recording is somewhat shorter than most, (especially when compared with the Goldstein version, which lasts over 1 hour 52 minutes), but my choice was informed by Takahashi's tone, rhythmic consistency and articulation of phrases. (The second recording by Fafchamps is also, in my opinion, quite excellent in this respect but was not available to me at the time of writing.)*

Whilst listening to the piece and making notes, I resisted the temptation to pause the CD player and did not refer to the score until I started to write up my notes the following day. As a result, there were times when the chronology of events became confused or where my descriptions of the materials differed slightly from what was indicated in the score. There were also occasions, perhaps adding up to a few minutes, when I found myself unable to write at all, immersed in the experience of pure listening. These hesitations and seeming contradictions have been preserved, wherever possible, in the completed text below, since a far from clear account of the work could be considered integral to Feldman's attempt to consciously disorientate the listener. I did allow myself the liberty, however, of re-writing certain phrases or passages that appeared inarticulate or unintelligible, and added to the original script where I felt there was room to describe what I had experienced in more detail. For instance, my original notes made reference to Merleau-Ponty's

OVERCOMING FORM: REFLECTIONS ON IMMERSIVE LISTENING

phenomenological views on time but my speculations were brief and needed to be re-examined and expanded upon for this final version. I have since made further minor revisions to the text as a whole (including adding a few pitch indications from the score), but hopefully have managed to preserve my thoughts and feelings from what now seems like a rather intense hour or so of listening. Needless to say, I felt it necessary to avoid expanding upon the text by going back and listening to the piece again. The 'of the moment' aspect of that initial listening experience was something that seemed essential to preserve if I was to capture some of the integrity of what Feldman brings to the compositional act itself.

I am not sure that I am the 'ideal' Feldman listener. I know the late pieces well and so my judgement is inevitably coloured by my understanding of other works from this period as well as my knowledge of Triadic Memories *itself. Also, at the time of writing I am engaged in research into extended duration in experimental works of this kind and so it is inevitable that a few key words, phrases and quotations on my mind that might just as well apply to other works will have found their way into the text. However, it had been some time since I last heard* Triadic Memories *in its entirety (Philip Thomas's performance at the University of Huddersfield in October 2010) and I was surprised whilst listening to the piece again how much of the material seemed new or different to what I remembered. This may have been partly due to not having heard Takahashi's version from start to end before. I am also aware that transcribing one's experiences is not an ideal way to appreciate this music and that having to commit my observations to the page must have had an effect on my mode of listening. Perhaps the main reason, however, is that there is so much in* Triadic Memories *to remember (or rather to forget). The notes below are testament to the sheer incomprehensibility of this work through the intentional confusion of memory protention and retention over its extended time scale.*

Through the process of retrospectively comparing my observations with the score, it has been interesting to observe how Triadic Memories *contains the genesis of many of the procedural aspects adopted by Feldman in subsequent works, and in particular* String Quartet II, *where the constant interplay of mobile materials over long periods of time becomes integral to our understanding of the work. From my notes below it seems clear that a disorientation of sorts occurs quite early on in the work (some three minutes in), where, due to a process of octave transposition, the close proximity of pitches within the three note cells makes it unclear where one motif ends and the next one begins. (Catherine Costello Hirata also discusses this perceptual illusion in her perceptive article 'G Maybe-To G#' (2005-2006, 383-385). However, it is from page 16 onwards that the real perceptive disorientation that Feldman discusses takes hold. It is at this point (just under 20 minutes in the Takahashi version) that Feldman begins to bring back previously heard material. The repetition of these same ideas continues throughout the next third of the piece, sometimes repeating ideas exactly but most often with some kind of variation. In the final third of the work new materials are introduced that are subsequently repeated in much the same way and also include elements from earlier in the composition. The idiosyncratic use of notation does not always translate audibly from the score (grace notes suspended in the air or repeats that are placed in the middle of bars for instance) but instead seem to provide some kind of mnemonic reference for the composer through which the same materials can be repeated, varied or combined. The lack of visual clues adds to this disorientation and is further complicated by the consistency of the pitch materials themselves (an abundance of seconds, sevenths and diminished fifths) that negates any immediate sense of directionality or functionality.*

Robert Henderson, following the British premiere of the work, described the piece as 'concerned with the shape of a leaf and not the tree' (1981). The following text very much expresses this viewpoint, focusing on the singular event, the solitary moment, through which form dissolves and scale opens up as real, experiential entity. One senses that Feldman discovered this for himself through years of composing and, no doubt, through listening to his own works. This act of discovery becomes something that we are invited to share in as a listener. This is not music that professes to provide answers but instead leaves us feeling enriched from the experience of listening.

OVERCOMING FORM: REFLECTIONS ON IMMERSIVE LISTENING

Quietly, persistently, an alternation of three-note figures
One figure *[G, G#, D]*, and then the other *[B♭, A, C#]*
Each note has its own weight
Like Mondrian, '*not painting bouquets, but single flowers at a time*' (Feldman 1985, 124)
Slightly irregular in periodicity but not entirely unpredictable
'*…the human face: overall symmetry dominates, but the halves, whilst internally consistent are not exactly the same*' (Glassie 1993, 671)
The repeated minor third *[G, B♭]* in the high register, floating
Pitted against the fog of the lower notes
Half-pedalled, distinguishable, but always slightly out of reach

Now a change in register as the highest notes descend by an octave
The same figure now plotted in a different space but with the same slight irregularity
Feldman's notion of a 'crippled symmetry', imbued with a playful ambiguity
These new notes, now considerably more foregrounded, step forward, assert themselves

Another registral shift as the lowest notes move up the octave, coming into focus, inhabiting the same space, becoming figurative, almost motivic
No, they now appear as distinct voices, locked into a continuity of pitches
Partial melodies conjoin and I no longer know where the patterning begins
Does the sequence start with the highest note and move downwards or vice-versa?
It is difficult to tell; an Escher staircase, traversed in both directions

And now the pitches change *[G, G♭, F]*
Notes chosen seemingly for the way in which they hang, immobile in the air
The rhythmic structure remains momentarily preserved and the patterning continues

Rotations, a confusion of the auditory senses
The music suddenly blossoms, like an opening flower
We are in a different space
The logic of the preceding moment is broken
A rich texture emerges, dancing between registers
An abundance of dyads, chords and arpeggios play in quick succession
[In the score these passages are notated across three staves]
Feldman has made the leap, his faith in intuition restored
I give up the promise of a continuing process
The suggestion that the piece, up and running, will write itself, was an illusion

Feldman does not allow us time to ruminate on how this textural interplay relates to the processional temporal unfolding of the preceding moment – we are in a new space
Chords, patterns, unfolding sumptuously

Now single patterns, repeated several times, obsessively
Four times, five times? They seem to vary
For a moment the music feels replenished, figurative once more
Still displaying such an abundance of unresolved tensions, Feldman keeps us attentive to the moment
If the music is to let up then that time is still to come

Figures and more figures
Changing patterns that appear flitting and spacious
A sound-world harmonically and texturally reminiscent of Takemitsu's late piano works or perhaps Jasper Johns' cross-hatch patterns; *Usuyuki*, *Dancers on a Plane*
Takahashi's patterns are light to the touch, yet etched decisively
'She slowly paints, lightning-quick apparitions' (Paz 1990, 46)

OVERCOMING FORM: REFLECTIONS ON IMMERSIVE LISTENING

Vertical material now dominates and a new moment emerges
I feel, temporarily, like I have arrived somewhere, but where?
The music seems to have lacked the directional impetus to have taken me here
An absence of musical grammatology, teleology, rhetoric
Now more cross-hatch patterns and the moment becomes seemingly more spacious

Rivulets of notes, repeated four or five times
A dialectical interplay now opens between chords inhabiting different registral spaces and fleeting patterns
These feel familiar, or at least seem to contain semblances of the past
Backwards, forwards, I had failed to notice previously how much Feldman likes to alternate between two events
More figures that vary in harmonic content but always the same highest note
A point of fixity on a traversed plane

Now, out of nowhere, a theme *[B, D♭ A#, D]*
When we talk of figures it is in relationship to a ground
But here, unaccompanied – a figure without a ground
Each note is stated independently, serenely; Proust's 'incandescent body'
Takahashi's touch – a reminder of what Feldman learnt from Madame Press
And from this comes a series of dyads, equally as sensuous to the touch
Shifting in registration

This see-sawing effect goes on for some time – a theme, then dyads
Feldman allows us to settle in the moment; to-ing and fro-ing
We revel in the beauty of the moment, alive to the sound
Like Beckett – always saying the same thing, backwards and forwards, *in and out of shadows*
Periodic, now a-periodic, saturated in hues

LISTENING THROUGH MORTON FELDMAN'S TRIADIC MEMORIES

I begin to see a spacious dimension opening up within the piece
A sense of wholeness through which the past does not beckon
It is becoming difficult to write or to describe the passing of events
Time seems to slow down
The sanctity of the moment
Feldman declares a space and invites me simply to listen

Now the remnants of this theme, and my memory involuntarily opens up
Is this presented too soon perhaps?
I do not wish to recall past events but to savour the moment
I remind myself that this past theme *is* now reinstated in the present

But this moment is fleeting and is now followed by a new event
An irregular arpeggiated figure, like the patter of rain
Close registration this time; clouded hues of minor thirds and semi-tones
Now high registration chords again and mid-to-low patterns
More ominous this time and even slower
Stretched out in time

Rising arpeggios, once again characterised by the same highest notes
More patterns, figures, always figures
Now persistent, obstinate, repetitive

The theme, each note presented individually, reinstated with each successive moment
Takahashi's tone – Madame Press at the piano
This seems to mark a new point in time and with it a different sonic world
I do not count the repetitions since this would leave a trace, suggest a path that points backwards
Somehow each sound seems like a new entity
How many times I hear each note I do not wish to know

OVERCOMING FORM: REFLECTIONS ON IMMERSIVE LISTENING

What purpose would it serve?
More broken textures, Takemitsu again
The single notes from the theme return and remind us of the beauty of touch
I anticipate a rising major third at the end of the melody but instead Feldman writes a chord
Momentarily I lost the moment, caught in anticipation

Now the theme, this time higher, half remembered
Feldman consciously evokes memory

An interruption through the persistence of a chordal passage in the mid-register
Its rhythmic periodicity and sense of contrary motion is clear and distinct
I break from the past, its memory momentarily erased
Now a reminder – patterns again with repeated high notes
Followed by clusters once more, always persistent, repetitive

After some time, figurations, more patterns
Obsessively repeating, almost familiar
Patterns and more patterns, the weave of the Anatolian rug maker
But I am lost. I cease to understand the relationships between the events I am hearing
I must simply submit to the moment
Unknowingly, perhaps, I cope through forgetting to remember

What I experience is not an intellectual art but requires the discipline to listen
My listening begins when I leave my analytical mind at the door
At the same time, Feldman is a realist; his art does not transport me to some fantastical realm –
Feldman is with me in the room, working, making those snap decisions

that keep me alive to the moment
It is difficult to continue to write, to describe this ongoing process, and I now know why most analysis of Feldman's music stops after the first few pages of the score
What I am witnessing is the constant interplay or rotation of maybe four of five ideas; clusters, patterns, repeated dyads, triads. What else?

Back a few pages, now forwards, back a little more
For me to describe these events over and over again seems redundant as an idea

I have been here before, looking back through the many pages of *String Quartet II* to find out where events re-occur
What can I say of this constant teasing out of ideas?
I have studied the score to *Triadic Memories* but right now its details elude me
Again, the failure of memory. What do I remember?
A handful of notational images, distinct yet inter-related
But here, in this 'acoustic reality' of the moment these notational images are somehow less apparent

This visual identity, these figures that inhabit the mind, seem richer and more textured, perhaps?
I want to see the score but that is to trick the ear into believing
Architectural, instrumental, spatial, three-dimensional
Communicative, yet beyond the realm of actual visual portrayal

Where am I? Perhaps only a third of the way through the piece but already writing less of the particulars of each event
What I wish to avoid at this point is some kind of narrative – *this*, then *this*, then *this*
The stark reality is quite different; I am inside something large, vacuous,

OVERCOMING FORM: REFLECTIONS ON IMMERSIVE LISTENING

transformative
This does not follow *this* that follows *this*
Each moment feels individual, marked by the passage of time perhaps, but equally unique
The opening of the piece – some time event in the past that I am not asked to recollect
The ending cannot exist since it does not equate with the conditions of my presence
It is not something that can be wholly imagined *right now* since it is something that has not yet occurred

[Merleau-Ponty reminds us that the analogy of time as a river containing a temporal flow has its limitations from an experiential point of view since this pre-supposes a witness who was there at its inception, and will continue to be there through its successive flow to the present and on into the future (Merleau-Ponty 1962, 411). On the other hand, when listening to a piece of music it might be considered that we do bear witness to the successive unfolding of the events in the work and follow its marked progress through time. And yet, in the case of Feldman's music, we might say that Merleau-Ponty's phenomenological view still seems to hold true; this time is not a continuation of that time. Nor is it that time reinstated. Right now, listening to the constant re-ordering of materials, it does not even feel like I am revisiting the same places. Rather, these are unique places that become 'habitable' through an understanding of some of the characteristics of the previous places. It is, as Feldman has stated elsewhere, like re-acquainting yourself with someone you have not seen for some time – we speak of knowing the person but with the knowledge that this person has changed through the experience of their recent past. They are simply not the same person ...]

But I digress ...

What I am witnessing, presently, within this large, outstretched moment,

is the alternation of two principal sets of materials:
The first comprises a single line with additional notes that flit and dance in quick successive leaps; the second, dyads that alternate between a mid and low range
This alternation, this coming and going, continues
An obsessive gesture emerges, repeated perhaps six or seven times
Now patterns previously heard again
But from which point in the past are they derived?
Are these the same pitch patterns or varied? Are the rhythmic profiles the same?
Does any of this really matter from an experiential perspective?
There are simply too many moments to keep track
And now, at a point when words fail me, Feldman introduces new material …

High notes and low notes leap agilely onto mid-range chords
Pairings of chords again – first *this*, then *that*
Each two-chord progression proceeded by a pause, then repeated
Once again, my memory seems to be wiped clean
A sonorous line emerges amongst the flitting of grace notes, elegantly conceived
Now, once again, the to-ing and fro-ing
Dyads again, this time a more abrasive type of patterning
The event feels familiar and yet somehow obscured
Transformed by its immediate past
A mid-range pattern
Again, the hue, the *abrash*

What follows *is* new but does not come entirely as a shock
The previous pitches give way to a single-line melody
Again unaccompanied, simple to the touch
No octave displacement here, just simple notes, contingently placed

OVERCOMING FORM: REFLECTIONS ON IMMERSIVE LISTENING

A stark melody *[D♭, C, D, C, E♭ etc.]* in the mid-range of the piano
Stretching out in time, a line taken for a walk
Then another new event – beautifully crisp, arpeggiated figures, reiterated again and again
Then the single-line melody
And the elegant arpeggios once more

The single-line melody returns again, this time in a new register
Octave shifts, reminiscent of the opening process
An indirect memory
But this is a new space

A brief dancing display of notes, simultaneously high and low
And now a surprise – a low tremelando passage
A rumble on a single chord, static, undefined
This moment becomes extended in time
The material feels uncharacteristic of Feldman
No, it is not the material that is uncharacteristic but the manneristic ('unfigurative') way in which Feldman presents it
A stranger in a room of figures
Will this return?
Where are we going? Where is the music taking us?

Stability is regained
Beautiful ripples that seem to emanate outwards against a silent backdrop
And now motionless chords that stand as stationary objects
Repeated without deviation in pitch or register
The same chords, played over and over, as if placed in a room to be observed singularly
We have come so far to observe the beauty of such simple things

Then repeated chords in various registers
Playful, colourful
Registration again
I sense the end of the piece. Why?

No, this is not the end.
But where are we?
Ripples again, figures, chords
Rotations that appear to look backwards and forwards
Everything against a white canvas
No pictorial depth, just surface
Mondrian's bouquets again, still life
Fixed chords, then ripples
Extended patterns
Motionless; Feldman suspends time in the air

More fixed chords, repetitious, solid to the touch
Now the single-line melody in a low registration
Pitch becomes almost obsolete against the hue
Except for single high notes that hover above, suspended in the air
A pause and then the melody again, now lower, stretched in time

Four notes [C, D, E♭, D♭], remnants of the theme
Now the fleeting arpeggios, separated by silence
In a moment they are gone and with it the piece
No conclusion, no ending, just another opening – this time onto the world
What can we draw from it all?
I cannot say, I am simply consumed by the silence from which the piece came

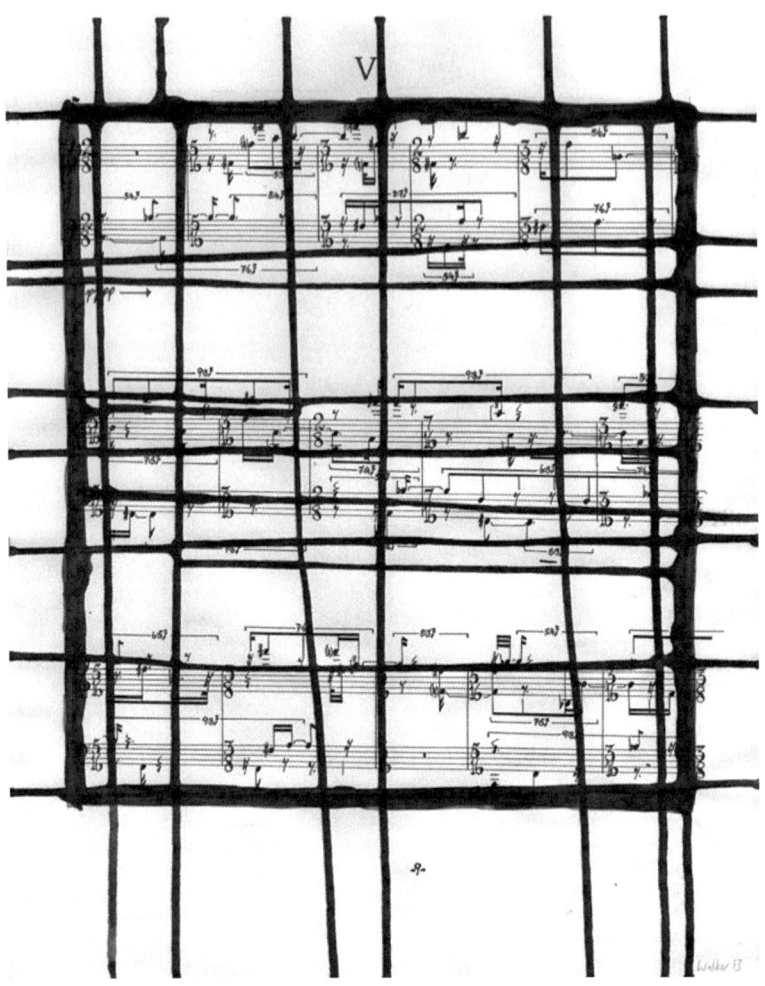

© Mike Walker 2013

Bibliography

Barry, R. 2013. 'Falling and Laughing: A Conversation with Pauline Oliveros'. *Fact*. Accessed 28 August 2013. http://www.factmag.com/2013/01/25/falling-and-laughing-a-conversation-with-pauline-oliveros/.

Beuger, A. 2001. 'calme etendue (spinoza)'. Sleeve notes: Edition Wandelweiser Records EWR 0107.

Bridget Riley. Directed by David Thompson. London: Arts Council of Great Britain, 1979. DVD.

Burr, A. 2012. 'Between Composition and Phenomena: Interpreting "In Memoriam John Higgins"'. *Leonardo Music Journal* 22. Online supplement. Accessed 6 September 2013. http://www.mitpressjournals.org/doi/abs/10.1162/LMJ_a_00107.

Clements, A. 2011. 'Naldjorlak – review'. *The Guardian*. 23 June. Accessed 28 August 2013. http://www.theguardian.com/music/2011/jun/23/eliane-radigue-naldjorlak-review.

Clifton, T. 1983. *Music as Heard: A Study in Applied Phenomenology*. New Haven: Yale University Press.

Colpitt, F. 1990. *Minimal Art: The Critical Perspective*. Seattle: University of Washington Press.

Curtis, C. n.d.. 'Naldjorlak'. Garden Variety. Accessed 22 August 2013. http://www.gardenvariety.org/projects/radigue/notes.html.

Curtis, C. 2012. 'Alvin Lucier: A Performer's Notes'. *Leonardo Music Journal* 22. Online supplement. Accessed 6 September 2013. http://www.mitpressjournals.org/doi/abs/10.1162/LMJ_a_00111.

Dax, M. 2012. 'Eliane Radigue: An Interview'. Electronic Beats. Accessed 28 August 2013. http://www.electronicbeats.net/en/features/interviews/eliane-radigue-an-interview/.

Demers, J. 2010. *Listening Through the Noise: The Aesthetic of Experimental Electronic Music*. New York: Oxford University Press.

Deleuze, G. 2004. *Difference and Repetition*. London: Continuum.

Deforce, A. 2008. 'Morton Feldman Patterns In A Chromatic Field'. Accessed 5 August 2013. *http://www.cnvill.net/mfdeforce.pdf.*

Farneth 1996. 'La Monte Young – Marian Zazeela: Ultra Modernist Minimalists'. *Metrobeat*. 22 April 22. Available at MELA Foundation, accessed 28 August 2013 http://www.melafoundation.org/farneth.htm.

Feldman, M. 2000. *Give My Regards To Eighth Street*, edited by B. H. Friedman. Cambridge, MA: Exact Change.

Frey, J. 2004. 'And on it went'. Accessed 6 June 2013. http://www.timescraper.de/_juerg-frey/texts-e.html.

Gann, K. n.d. 'Naldjorlak'. Garden Variety. Accessed 22 August 2013. http://www.gardenvariety.org/projects/radigue/bio.html.

Gilmore, B. 2006. 'Wild Air: The Music of Kevin Volans'. *Journal of Music*, 1 November. Accessed 7 August 2013. http://journalofmusic.com/focus/wild-air-music-kevin-volans.

Glassie, H. 1993. *Turkish Traditional Art Today*. Bloomington: Indiana University Press.

Grimshaw, J. 2011. *Draw a Straight Line and Follow It: The Music and Mysticism of La Monte Young*. New York: Oxford University Press.

Hanninen, D. A. 2004. 'Feldman, Analysis, Experience'. *twentieth century music* 1(2): 225–51.

Harrison, B. 2013. 'Scanning the temporal Surface: Aspects of time, memory and repetition in my recent music'. *Divergence Press* 1. Accessed 7 August 2013. http://www.divergencepress.com/Journal/JournalIssue/tabid/85/ID/8/Scanning-the-temporal-surface-aspects-of-time-memory-and-repetition-in-my-recent-music.aspx.

Henderson, R. 1981 'Morton Feldman's Triadic Memories'. Accessed 7 August 2013. http://www.cnvill.net/mfjack.htm.

Hirata, C. 2005 'G Maybe-To G#'. *Perspectives of New Music, 43/44: 378-402.*

Ihde, D. 2007. *Listening and Voice: Phenomenologies of Sound*. 2nd edn. New York: State University of New York Press.

Janatjeva, V. 2006. 'Rytis Mažulis' ajapajapam in Huddersfield'. Music Export Lithuania. Accessed 28 August 2013. http://www.mic.Lt/en/info/212.

Kramer, J. 1988. *The Time of Music*. New York: Schirmer.

LaBelle, B. 2006. *Background Noise: Perspectives on Sound Art*. New York: Continuum.

Le Poidevin, R. 1991. *Change, Cause and Contradiction: A Defence of the Tenseless Theory of Time*. Basingstoke: Palgrave Macmillan.

Lippard, L. R., ed. 1968. 'Questions to Stella and Judd'. In *Minimal Art: A Critical Anthology*, edited by G. Battcock, 136–54. Toronto: Dutton.

Merleau-Ponty, M. 1962. *Phenomenology of Perception*. London: Routledge.

Majmon, M. O. 2005. 'Analysis of Morton Feldman's String Quartet No.2 (1983)'. Accessed 23 June 2013. http://www.cnvill.net/mfolsen_english.pdf.

Morris, R. 1966. 'Notes of Sculpture'. In *Minimal Art: A Critical Anthology*, edited by G. Battcock, 222–35. Toronto: Dutton.

Noë, A. 2006. *Action in Perception*. Cambridge: MIT Press.

Oliveros, P. 2005. *Deep Listening: A Composer's Sound Practice*. Lincoln: Deep Listening Publications.

Paton, S. 2009. 'Time-*Lessness*, simultaneity and successivity: repetition in Beckett's short prose'. *Language and Literature* 18(4). Accessed 6 September 2013. http://lal.sagepub.com/content/18/4/357.short

Paz, O. 1990. *Alternating Current*. Translated by H. Lane. New York: Arcade Publishing

Pisaro, M. 2009. 'Wandelweiser'. erstwords. 23 September. Accessed 28 August 2013. http://erstwords.blogspot.co.uk/2009/09/wandelweiser.html.

Paccione, P. 2010 'For Christian Wolff (review)'. *American Music* 28(1). Accessed 5 August 2013. http://muse.jhu.edu/journals/amm/summary/v028/28.1.paccione.html.

Quinn, I. 2006. 'Minimal Challenges: Process Music and the Uses of Formalist Analysis'. *Contemporary Music Review* 25(3): 283–94.

Rockwell, J. 1999 'Morton Feldman (and Crippled Symmetry)'. Accessed 5 August 2013. http://www.cnvill.net/mfrockwl.htm.

Saunders, J. 2003. 'Developing a modular approach to music'. PhD diss. University of Huddersfield.

Saunders, J. 2009. *The Ashgate Companion to Experimental Music*. Aldershot: Ashgate Publishing Limited.

Smith, A. 2011. 'Light, Space, Colour: The Impact of Abstract Visual Stimuli on the Aesthetic of Kevin Volans'. Dublin Instuitute of Technology. Accessed 6 November 2012. http://arrow.dit.ie/aaconmusbk/1/.

Snyder, B. 2000. *Music and Memory: An Introduction.* Cambridge, MA: MIT Press.

Szlavnics, C. 2006. 'Opening Ears – the Intimacy of the Detail of Sound'. *Filigrane: Nouvelles Sensibilités* 4: 37–57.

Tenney, J. 1988. *Meta + Hodos and META Meta + Hodos.* 2nd edn. n.p.: 1988.

Villars, C., ed. 2006. *Morton Feldman Says.* London: Hyphen Press.

Voegelin, S. 2010. *Listening to Noise and Silence: Towards a Philosophy of Sound Art.* London: Continuum.

Winship, J. 2010. 'Eliane Radigue'. Sparks in Electric Jelly. Accessed 28 August 2013. http://sparksinelectricaljelly.blogspot.co.uk/2010/03/eliane-radigue.html.

Wolff, D. n.d. 'Alvin Lucier'. Material Press. Accessed 28 August 2013. http://www.materialpress.com/lucier.htm.

Wyse, P. 2011. 'Eliane Radigue's Brave New Worlds'. *The Guardian.* 16 June. Accessed 28 August 2013. http://www.guardian.co.uk/music/2011/jun/16/eliane-radigue-electronic-music interview?INTCMP=SRCH.

Young, G. 1978. 'Gayle Young interviews James Tenney'. *Only Paper Today* 5(5).

Young, L. M. 1965. 'Lecture 1960'. *The Tulane Drama Review* 10(2): 73–83.

Recommended Listening

Peter Adriaansz: Waves
Wave 3, Waves 5-7
Ensemble Klang
Ensemble Klang records EKCD1 (2010)

Antoine Beuger
calme étendue (spinoza)
Antoine Beuger, Sprechstimme
Edition Wandelweiser Records EWR 0107 (2001)

Morton Feldman: Triadic Memories
Aki Takahashi, piano
ALM Records ALCD-33 (1989)

Morton Feldman: Triadic Memories
Jean-Luc Fafchamps, piano
Sub Rosa SR280 (2011)

Morton Feldman: String Quartet (II)
Ives Ensemble
Hat[now]ART 4-144 (2001)

Morton Feldman: For Samuel Beckett
Klangforum Wien, cond. Sylvain Cambreling
Kairos KAI0012112 (1999)

OVERCOMING FORM: REFLECTIONS ON IMMERSIVE LISTENING

transference
Bryn Harrison: *Surface Forms (repeating)*
ELISION
Huddersfield Contemporary Records HCR02 (2010)

Bryn Harrison: Vessels
Philip Thomas, piano
Another Timbre At69 (2013)

Alvin Lucier
In Memoriam John Higgins, *In Memoriam Stuart Marshall*, and *Charles Curtis*
Anthony Burr, clarinet, and Charles Curtis, cello
ANTIOPIC ANSI002 (2005)

Alvin Lucier: Crossings
Wesleyan University New World Consort
Lovely Music LCD 1018 (1990)

Rytis Mažulis: Cum Essem Parvulus
Ajapajapam
Latvian Radio Chamber Singers
Megadisc 7810 (2004)

Phill Niblock: Touch Three
Sethwork and *Valence*
Seth Josel and Julia Eckhardt
Touch records TO:69 (2006)

Phill Niblock: Disseminate
Disseminate Ostrava
Ensemble OCNM
Mode 131 (2004)

RECOMMENDED LISTENING

Eliane Radigue: Trilogie De La Mort
Kyema, *Kailasha* and *Koumé*
Experimental Intermedia Foundation XI 119 (1998)

Howard Skempton: Canons + Hoquets
Tendrils
Quatour Bozzini
Collection QB CQB 0704 (2007)

Old School: James Tenney
Critical Band and *Harmonium #2*
Zeitkratzer
Zeitkratzer records ZKR0010 (2010)

Kevin Volans: Cicada
Cicada
Jill Richards and Mathilda Hornsveld, pianos
Black Box B00004SSJQ (2000)

Wandelweiser und so weiter
A 6-CD box set of music in, around or near that of the composers in the Wandelweiser collective
Another Timbre At56x6 (2012)

Biographies

Richard Glover is a composer based in Huddersfield, where he completed his PhD investigating perception and cognition within music of sustained tone textures. He is currently a lecturer in composition at Huddersfield, and researches the perception, construction and notation of experimental musics. He has written book chapters on the music of Phill Niblock and the role of technology in minimalist music, and is currently working on publications concerning the temporal experience in experimental music. His portrait cd Logical Harmonies was released on the 'another timbre' label in October 2013.

Bryn Harrison is a composer and a senior lecturer at the University of Huddersfield from where he was awarded a PhD by Publication in 2007. He has established a close working relationship with many international ensembles including Ensemble Plus-Minus, ELISION, Apartment House, Asamisimasa, Exaudi and the London Sinfonietta. His recent output has seen the further development of recursive musical structures with a series of compositions of long duration such as the 45' ensemble work *repetitions in extended time* (2008) and the 76' solo piano piece *Vessels* (2012/13) available on the 'another timbre' label in October 2013.

Mike Walker is a painter, printmaker, teacher and writer based in Chichester in the South East of England. He has exhibited widely including solo exhibitions at Claremont Studios, Hastings, The Bowery, Leeds and Abbot Hall Gallery, Kendal as well as numerous group exhibitions. He has a strong interest in contemporary music and has undertaken several collaborations, principally with the composer Bryn Harrison including in 2006 Music for a

OVERCOMING FORM: REFLECTIONS ON IMMERSIVE LISTENING

Light Room / Music for a Dark Room, Exeter Phoenix, commissioned for tEXt 06, Exeter. He is presently an Associate Lecturer at the Universities of Kent and Chichester. More recently he has begun to write pieces for other artists. He lives in Chichester with his wife and son.